The Endangered Species?

How Evolution and New Age Spiritual Families Can Save Humankind

By

Geoffrey Luff Stocker

Edited by

Christine Stocker Gibson

About the Author

Geoffrey Luff Stocker (2 July 1923 – 23 January 2005), formerly a consultant chemist, a ventriloquist and member of the Magic Circle, was ordained as Deacon in the Free Protestant Episcopal church, gaining both a research fellowship and doctorate in the 1960s.

His underlying interest in the field of personal psychology led him to found the Hampstead School of Speech and Drama and The School of Psychological Salesmanship, subsequently founding The Sleep Learning Association, for which he authored the Geoffrey Stocker Tapes and a monthly journal, as well as contributing to other hypnotherapy and hypnopaedia publications.

ISBN: 9798631318076

Table of Contents

Foreword

Existential questions about humankind's origins, its purpose on Earth, its relationship with the divine and debates about its future have exercised curious intellects and different faiths for millennia, and the subject continues to invite healthy debate across a variety of related philosophies: destiny versus self-determination, mankind's spiritual dependence on gods versus its own omnipotence, Evolution versus Creationism, the ethics surrounding human biological engineering and neuroscience.

Geoffrey Luff Stocker, the author of many psychology publications and the originator of the writings in this book, had a deep fascination with human behaviour all his career, in particular with psychological therapies. Whilst initially qualifying as an analytical chemist, he was strongly drawn to the world of behavioural psychology and spent many years researching ways in which the unconscious could be used to manipulate and enhance personal development, resulting in a diverse professional career as a magician and ventriloquist, as a voice coach and drama teacher, and as a person-centred therapist.

In the late 1970s and early 1980s, an emerging social phenomenon crossed the Atlantic from America: a therapeutic self-help and counselling culture providing a new exciting trajectory for professionals in those fields in the UK. These were heady days and, by 1984, Geoffrey had founded the School of Psychological Salesmanship, based in London but with an international reach, which provided him with a broad client base for continuing his research. Those writings have been heavily referenced in Chapter 4 of this book. During this time he qualified as a hypnotherapist and while supporting people seeking to significantly change their lives with established therapeutic interventions, he also believed that hypnotherapy, particularly hypnopaedia, could valuably be used to assist individuals' learning. This led to the formation of an innovative learn-while-you-sleep programme, co-authorship of several publications on hypnopaedia and the creation of a range of sleep-learning study tapes. Thus was the Sleep Learning Foundation born: a study centre in London with dormitories in the rural serenity of the New Forest in Hampshire, where students enhanced their learning capacity while they slept.

Geoffrey was a deeply spiritual man who, in parallel with his therapeutic research, continued to seek his religious truths, this finally culminating in ordination in the Lutheran church. Crucially, for this book, the thesis for his divinity doctorate perfectly illustrated his belief in the power of the unconscious as evidence of a creative, divine intent that humankind be destined for the ultimate spiritual enlightenment, the manifestation of mankind's perfect evolution, which is expanded on in the opening chapter.

In the late 1990s, the last decade of the last millennium and in the autumn of his own life, he undertook his most ambitious research project, his swan song: a social commentary about mankind's place in the universe. He believed that evolution has brought humankind to The MidPoint, the turning point in the history of our civilisation, the time and place at which collective intellectual and spiritual understandings can be harnessed to take humankind to its next evolutionary stage, the New Age, that of total enlightenment, absolute knowledge.

Unexpectedly, he was never to complete this personal journey as he died in 2005 without completing the first draft of his book. Posthumously then, I, his daughter, have been familiarising myself with the mountain of notes he had handwritten and my hugest thanks must go to my good friend and desktop publisher, Linda Hadfield, for helping me type up the notes, edit and distil them into this book you are now reading.

And now, a word from Geoffrey to you...

"Having absolute knowledge means being aware of higher consciousness, an appreciation of the human mind,

understanding the purpose of our life. I propose that Evolution has pre-established philosophy establishing man with a destiny and with it a new desire to harness the unlimited powers of the mind, both conscious and unconscious. There is no limit to the knowledge we may absorb. Any blockages we have are just psychological."

Christine Stocker Gibson (editor), 2020

Introduction

Successful New Age living requires a seismic shift, a revolutionary approach to provide a mobile enough environment for families to grow and develop to become their best selves. None of us can become our best selves, or be an ambassador for our community or for the wider good, if the structure of our environment is rigid and in favour of an elite group of the population. Shaping a new and nurturing world is not a small undertaking. Our power structure, its economics and politics, its education, boundaries, its criminal legislation and the trajectory of its scientific and technical growth will either enable or constrict its potential.

As it is, with the clashing opposites of the pre-MidPoint world, social conflict is so easy to identify but less able to be resolved. Political and technological extremism creates tangled webs of misinformation and confusion which the perpetrators intend to project into the deepest midst of us all to achieve social breakdown, sometimes, powerful groups clashing one against the other to the detriment of social cohesion and balance. Many will live their lives posturing and scheming to inflict their terrible aims on us all and may end their lives within the violence and aggression it creates.

Our society needs to make urgent adjustments, even radical changes, to achieve even a relatively stable society, and because many changes are required in almost every department of our lives, it would be quite impossible for one book to provide sufficient comment. This, however, is my purpose and I am pleased to be a small part of a greater awareness as other more learned and brilliant minds expand on the areas of knowledge which have to be garnered and synthesise them to achieve a greater whole: a philosophy for shared living, for developing our humanity in a way that benefits both the planet and its peoples.

I consider myself a philosopher as well as a psychotherapist, concerned not only with the psychological problems of life but also with standards, values, principles and patterns of living.

Knowledge is essential in the first place so that imagination can take its rightful place in a new synthesis. There is, of course, not one single problem to be resolved but a multiplicity of them, of great complexity, which are challenging our civilisation and our social boundaries, which are exercising some of our greatest minds, across a range of disciplines at this very time. I believe the main reason for this rise in conflict is a lack of insight into the "unity of opposites".

I hope to show how the chaotic disorders which have caused crises in our civilisation are due to natural Evolutionary developments: unavoidable, as social standards, values and principles change. Mankind has a confused understanding about its place. We have knowledge of spiritual, metaphysical, psychological matters but have not yet found a way to transform these into a beneficial philosophy for life. A single mind cannot comprehend everything there is to know. All knowledge, whether creative, practical or academic, must now be integrated into the same great philosophy for living to enable man to achieve greater heights. Our great thinkers have, between them sufficient knowledge for this stage of man's development on planet Earth. That is our ultimate objective.

We have a tendency to want more and more information before committing ourselves when, in reality, we are sufficiently informed, to begin. Some may seek more knowledge, some seek more success, more money or more self-glory. When will we come together to put the pieces together, like a giant jigsaw puzzle, not separately but jointly creatively to acknowledge the continuing development of our whole civilisation, each discipline conveying knowledge, imagination, wisdom within its own specialism to illustrate the evolutionary benefits of achieving order, harmony, equilibrium?

Unity and orderliness of nature is not merely a New Age belief, or a new philosophy, even a new concept. We need not be a theologian, philosopher, psychologist or scientist to be affected by what we are observing or to devise solutions to our failings. Whilst the gaps in our scientific knowledge may be large and our ignorance very great, at this Mid-Point I believe they are shortening and inspiring of greater exploration; that we have sufficient knowledge (to begin to address the issues) and that to delay further would leave essential questions unresolved, and this chaos unbridled.

Man has natural desire to know what life is about although I am certain there is greater intent in the evolutionary processes of nature than we have realised. Divisiveness in man's responses to his quest for truth has gradually drawn him away from established religions and philosophical beliefs to an independent pragmatism, a reluctance to accept anything as true, unless it can be proved. More, even a belief that humankind itself is in control.

G.L.S.

Chapter 1
Evolution, The Intelligence and Our Unconscious

Twentieth century man, it is clear, needs a new organ for dealing with destiny, a new system of religious beliefs and attitudes adapted to the new situation in which his societies now have to exist. Earlier religions and belief-systems were largely adaptations to cope with man's ignorance and fears, with the result that they came to concern themselves primarily with stability of attitude. But the need today is for a belief-system adapted to cope with knowledge and creative possibilities, and this implies the capacity to meet, inspire and guide change. Evolutionary Humanism is a new organisation of ideas and potential action emerging from the present revolution of thought, is based on our understanding of Man and his relations with the rest of his environment, organised around the facts and ideas of evolution, taking account of the discovery that man is part of a comprehensive evolutionary process and cannot avoid playing a decisive role in it.

Julian Huxley, *Essays of a Humanist*, 1964

Ever since the publication of *The Origin of Species*, people have been pondering the significance of Evolution for the meaning of their lives, and of life in general. Are we a biological accident or a cosmic imperative? It poses the questions "Where is God's place if everything has a natural cause?" "Can Darwin's theory be supported theistically or atheistically?" For some people, the only way to deal with the question is to deny the evidence for Evolution altogether even as in the 1950s in the USA of the church suppressing their own scientists' leading research in the fields of palaeontology, genetics and zoology because of pressure from the creationist mainstream.

The debate continues. Is God the creator of all things, without whose continuous will for it to be so, nothing would exist? Consider this: if a God used and providentially controlled evolutionary mechanisms in the creation of plants and animals, there can be no reason to reject an evolutionary origin for humankind. Evolution affords plenty of room for God. Scientists would argue that mutations that make Evolution possible take place on a quantum level and, as a result, they can never know with perfect certainty whether a particular mutation will take place. Therefore, thanks to this uncertainty, if such a God can influence Evolution by initiating mutations His effects will be scientifically undetectable.

Conversely, in the 1970s and 80s it was posited by scientists James Lovelock and Lyn Margulis that the Earth as a whole can be seen as operating and evolving in ways analogous to a single organism: a self-regulating complex system involving the biosphere, atmosphere, hydrosphere and pedosphere - the soil cycle which operates on the earth's surface, creating conditions for the growth of green plants and hence the basis of the food cycle for all living organisms (*Gaia: A New Look at Life on Earth*, James Lovelock, 1979). They further argue that the interactions between the physical systems and living organisms contributed to the creation – and continue to maintain the existence – of a set of conditions closely adapted to the needs of living organisms.

Lovelock chose Gaia, the name of the Ancient Greek earth goddess (or personification of "Mother Nature"), to describe this planetary "super-organism", and subsequent writers have adopted this name and concept to argue that this homeostatic balance is purposefully pursued in order to maintain the optimal conditions for life on Earth. Aldo Leopold, pioneer in the development of modern environmental ethics and the movement for wilderness conservation likewise proposed a "living Earth" as central to his biocentric ethical approach:

"It is at least not impossible to regard the earth's parts – soil, mountains, rivers, atmospheres, etc - as organs or parts of organs of a coordinated whole, each part with its definite function. And, if we could see this whole as a whole, through a great period of time, we might perceive

not only organs with coordinated functions, but possibly also that process of consumption as replacement, which in biology we call metabolism, or growth. In such case, we would have all the visible attributes of a living thing, which we do not realise to be such because it is too big and its life processes too slow." (Aldo Leopold, *A Sand County Almanac*, 1949).

My premise is that the universe, whether or not constructed by God, functions beautifully using natural laws. We may comprehend Evolution's creation as His divine plan but equally we may say Evolution has created us to give us freedom to make our own future.

My approach is neither theist nor atheist, it is deist: that, whether or not constructed by God, Evolution set in motion the universe to unroll in the way it has, and does, and my premise is that Evolution has the universe's destiny embedded within it and that humankind is just one part of that plan. I believe that we are now living at the MidPoint of Evolution, a pivotal time which affords humankind the opportunities to embrace and accelerate its humanity, its learning and its spirituality, to help create a future worthy of succeeding generations.

MidPoint is then the turning point in the history of our civilisation when the powerful, and sometimes colliding, philosophies of the world's religions meet face on with the scientific community's ambitions for humankind to expand its potential, perhaps even surpass it with the aid of the new neurosciences and biotechnology. What is humankind's purpose? Is it to manage creation, perhaps to become divine itself and take control of the evolutionary process, even though it has yet to perfect an aspirational universal model for mortal living?

In this book, I hope to illuminate the capacity of infinite enlightenment, which is freely available to all those who seek it, by explaining the Philosophy of the Unconscious, a homage to the inevitability and indestructibility of Evolution and the opportunity that we, humankind, have as the instrument, or medium, for this spiritual expression.

I hope to show that a philosophy, or supreme plan, is operating in the unconscious, the so-called irrational part of man, and that this plan has been responsible for a significant part of our being: our moral values. Moral, ethical and spiritual values cannot be overlooked if man is to be fully examined and fully developed. From the time of birth, perhaps even before, what happens to man can influence what happens in man. Such a plan with a certain creative continuity, existing as humankind lives within its diverse groupings, has created and sustains such certain moral values.

I contend that our Unconscious has a pre-established philosophy establishing man with a destiny, and not "free will" and that these moral valuations are created by these recognised patterns of nature. I hope to show that this Philosophy of the

Unconscious, an intelligence driving operations, expressed by dynamic instinctive forces, is designed to allow the growth and development of humankind in relation to all other living organisms. This philosophy, because it has order and coordination, demonstrates that an underlying intelligence, with structures, is in place to achieve the transitional developments found in Evolution.

Man is a spiritual being, comprising energy and matter which became physical at some stage of the evolutionary programme. His environment has played a part in modifying his deep-rooted biological needs through the ages. For example, the self-preservation instinct recognised in all animals, including man, was greater in the days of greater ignorance and sparse population when man was less equipped to cope with his environment. In our contemporary, developed cultures, health services have eliminated fear from plagues and illnesses, and the instinct of self-preservation may never be aroused in man to such a degree again.

Humankind has natural desire to know what life is about and there is debate in the scientific world about man's impact on nature's Evolution, but it is notable that man's responses to his quest for truth have gradually drawn him away from established religions and philosophical beliefs to a secular scepticism, a reluctance to accept anything as true unless it can be proved. In matters of spirituality though, all which exists, exists as it is! Can you reject the existence of spirituality? Can love be proved to exist? Or happiness? None can deny their impact, however.

The great prophets of enlightenment had an intrinsic understanding of purity, beauty, sublime order and harmony of life. If the point of attaining higher knowledge is to stop the forward movement of our social fragmentation we should gather meticulously what we admire from all disciplines, for the greater advance of our civilisation and its entry into the New Age; to move from our social disunity towards a combined movement for growth and maturity.

The apparent, or conscious, physical world takes up almost all our attention, but vast invisible areas of our reality are simply ignored. Though much of man's past worldly ignorance has been overcome through widespread education, we now need to differentiate the great mass of knowledge available to us and see how it all interrelates within a great working whole. It is this which I refer to as The Intelligence, or as Evolution.

This MidPoint is a <u>red alert</u> stage in human evolution. Man must become aware of his soul; he must realise he <u>is</u> a soul. The definition of the soul is all that is <u>within</u> the physical self. We have given exaggerated importance to our corporeal selves. This is not just a religious conception, it is necessary evolutionary awareness.

Discovery of, release of, and development of the unrestricted potential of the soul of the individual is a flow-through from the Intelligence, understood as such, all to do with the unseen, invisible, vibrations or creative forces of Evolution, electro-dynamic forces from its source of origin.

There has been much dichotomy, so much polarisation, in almost every subject there is such squabbling confusion that the truth must be extricated from the conflicts – and the imperative for humankind, its first objective, is to prevent human annihilation! Far more knowledge is available to us than has been realised. Even if we accept that if such a cataclysmic end of humanity were to take place, Evolution would still continue, unperturbed, creatively progressing and expanding. Our descendants, should any survive, will look back with astonishment that we humans on this earth at this time were totally unable to cope with the affairs of the life we created; were too wayward, aggressively divided, not to plan to survive!

There are so many strands of opinion on almost all subjects because of the diversity of knowledge and experience that each of us has. We mistakenly divide everything up into seeming opposites of thought; we talk of good and bad, right and wrong, planning to do this and not that, and so on.

Dis-order, dis-ease, and all the mental and physical health illnesses, are negative symptoms of the pre-MidPoint stage – a painful transition stage.

The heightened general state of stress and tension and worry disorganises the metabolism. There is periodically an outbreak of a new disease that becomes an epidemic. Whilst drug therapy can have excellent results quite often, it is not the answer to the human dilemma. The cost of pre-MidPoint life is frighteningly colossal. The cost of human health, mentally, physically and spiritually is frighteningly enormous. The cost in money to control humans and social classes is vast being the cost of police, army, prison authority, legal administration, social care etc.

This is not a criticism, however. The pre-MidPoint stage in the growth of a civilisation is the most uncontrollable and traumatic of all stages. In this pre-MidPoint stage, we have lived an inexplicable life, not knowing why we are here, what we should be doing, or where we are going. Understanding is of course making itself known and will be profound, but it will be a long collective journey. That is why it is so important to understand the law of relativity, see things in perspective, to realise that Evolution goes in stages, that progress towards insight and wisdom goes slowly. What we can do is to get on with keen, sharp learning, using our vital senses on fully charged batteries to move from a state of collective ignorance to one of collective and selective wisdom.

It becomes vitally important that humankind takes responsibility for creating an enlightened, beneficial, universal model, with pathways for collaborations across the globe to share the best advancements and knowledge from all societies and cultures to inspire greater self-knowledge and aspiration within its populations. Failure to do so will be to miss the biggest challenge to humankind to provide a better future for itself and in so doing to slow the destabilisation of our world, both in old ways we do understand, and in new technological ways we have yet to fully comprehend.

You may be surprised then that I say our human problems are not crime, murder, political and military destructivity, atom bombs. These are but symptoms. The problem originates in the heart of man, his emotions not being sufficiently balanced. They produce counter-productive, non-harmonious, complex behaviours which culminate in anti-social, anti-human behaviours arising from emotions lacking focal direction due to ignorance of the real function of the human in the scheme of things. Mankind has been struggling with adverse attitudes and behaviours unaware of its role in the scheme of things, our love of life, love of ourselves, love of our creative self-expression, love of caring for others. Such powerful dynamic emotions must be integrated collectively in society to form the basis of a mature orderly post-MidPoint growth.

How do we find the order? How do we find the ease? How do we link with and integrate with The Intelligence, ie Evolution? How do we develop spiritual perfection within ourselves? It is by following the great programme of Evolution. There is

no need to resist the forces felt to be responsible for
pain and stress such as fate, God, our government,
our parents. If we could only understand the
wholeness of everything there is and our continuity in
the whole Evolutionary process, we would lose the
fears and insecurity which bring about deterioration
of the whole person. Evolution is in charge, whether
we like it or not, whether we realise it or not.

The ways of the post-MidPoint were totally
incomprehensible to man in his pre-MidPoint stage.
The ways needed for the New Age now might be
equally hard to comprehend. Usually knowledge is
developed gradually stage by stage, an evolutionary
movement from ignorance to knowledge but now at
this MidPoint all knowledge must be brought
together rapidly and embraced. Immediately. It needs
to become a revolution, a change so shocking that the
whole balance of life becomes an earthquake of all
feelings as the shift from ignorance to knowledge
arrives for us all at the same historic moment. In this
red alert, drop everything you are doing and take
action, for survival of the fittest is still the greatest law
of Evolution. Man will suddenly be aware of his past
ignorance - and the new knowledge will be
shattering!

The reason for this MidPoint is to make sense of
the whole universal programme and to realise and
enjoy our dynamic place in it. The key word of the
MidPoint is sufficiency. To understand it. To use it.
We are all at the now point in our personal evolution

and what we know will be sufficient for us, at this time.

Cause and Effect and the Problem of Opposites

Before we can begin to understand any aspect of life we must go back to the first principle. The Law of Cause and Effect, sometimes referred to as 'causation', operated at all times. It is an immutable universal law encompassing the principle that nothing in the universe can ever happen by chance. Every single effect within our world, upon our earth, has a cause, an original starting point. Unless we grasp the first principle all human thought will be pointless and useless.

Man is trying to shape his history, his destiny, but by not knowing just what wonderful resources he has for this objective, he is making a poor attempt, and sometimes the inevitable errors bring additional problems and complications which only induce further errors. Only by understanding the Laws of Evolution and what it means, quite apart from who or what is responsible for it, can one put the subject on a rational footing for proper investigation. There are obvious advantages in studying the various sciences, but the study of mental, emotional, spiritual realities, which follow exactly the same Laws of Evolution, has been an area of almost sheer neglect. The physical and materialistic matters occupy greater attention – because they can be seen and manipulated and sometimes with great skill - but the causal forces of

Evolution have been neglected. Only in the East do
they develop this most important subject.

Everything in the universe is ordered,
synchronised and in perfect evolving movement. You
were one tiny cell. Then you became two cells, then
four, eight, sixteen, thirty-two and so on. Because of
the great order of things, before you became one cell,
you did not start from zero. You evolved from what
went before. The Law of Cause and Effect, the driving
force, the initiating force of all time, was responsible.
This is indeed a force greater than we are, that always
was, always is and always will be. How is it we place
ourselves so high in the scheme of things? That is just
our own ego talking. The force that produced you
produces everything perfectly as it produced you
perfectly, cell by cell, and we are all part of the
environment, or life, or the universe: we are
interacting perpetually and perfectly with the whole
of creation as we were designed to do.

The glimpse of the error gives us the
appropriate enlightenment. Fundamentally we move
from uncertainty, confusion and ignorance towards
certainty – full awareness of reality in its wholeness,
restoration of the equilibrium of Evolution. Then each
of us will be functioning on previously unseen planes
in our fulfilled state, but as we progress, very, very
slowly indeed, for there is a lot to learn on the way,
we cannot understand enough generally to feel
satisfied with our very real and satisfactory position.
We have mixed feelings, opposing feelings, maybe

barely even satisfied, never feeling fully secure, often afraid of the future or with existing irrational fears. If there can be little full joy, love of life or love of self, we may feel impotent in the face of trying to "cope with it all". We will probably feel trapped and confused in a world of opposites, or conflicting emotions: feelings of love or hate, selfishness or generosity; adverse feelings if we imagine them to be "bad", pleasurable feelings if we imagine them to be "good". We flounder about with all kinds of mixed rules, laws, and multifarious –ologies and –isms, and utter confusion due to the ignorance about the opposites of good and bad, right and wrong, moral and immoral, greed and generosity, and so on.

A person might spend a whole day defending some theory with the greatest conviction, or spend energies on opposing some other theory that seems to threaten his status or ego, but with objective depth analysis it might be found that the person is influenced by personal prejudice, lack of sufficient knowledge, or irrational motivation, and might be entangled in the confusion caused by the opposites.

The opinions of many opposing critics might arise out of a similar set of false values. The reality might prove to be not that "I am right and you are wrong" with both having the same conviction but one opposed to the other, but rather "we are both wrong. We have failed to get down to the primary truth". The primary truth can only be located as a true fact of nature as part of the evolutionary programme, because Evolution is all that is. That is what we are all about, and that is what life is all about, and what everything is all about.

In politics, for example, the motivational force is often to win the election, to postulate one's point with all the power and confidence that can be conjured up; to never give up, to strive for the top, to be a success, and "may the best man win!" But this is an unconscious urge just as we see in poor lemmings as they all go over the cliff – any cliff – whichever cliff happens to be there at the time! In the human, this is not rational use of the creative mind, nor rational emotional behaviour. Politicians seldom have passionate desire to evaluate the Laws of Evolution, to discover first the requirements and harmonious creativity of nature as a guide to human behaviour, or order. We must <u>start</u> with each process of Evolution, scrutinise it, understand it, then see how all the laws are interrelated, and how we are interrelated to the whole of Evolution.

If this mature, rational approach is continually flouted, and if the confusions of the opposites are not sufficiently resolved, human progress to this potentially enlightened, intermediate stage, the MidPoint stage, will remain seriously hindered. At the present time there is much disordered thinking, and with it the ever-growing feeling of chaos and possible annihilation as we all fly off at different tangents, this way or that. A greater degree of order is now required which can only be achieved by rooting ourselves in the true facts of life, not notions, opinions, prejudices or superstitions. It is no use coming out with another "brilliant theory" however much it captures the imagination if the audience is comprised of confused people grasping for a solution. There are already red-herrings aplenty.

How, then, can our man-made laws be changed, maybe changed again, and even again to "get matters right"? Do they necessarily get right "right"? And then "right" for whom? For this person or that one? This party or that party? What is this "right" that we are all trying to find? Who is right? What is right? Little wonder that there is confusion, insecurity, disillusionment, and all our society's emotional disorders. Such is the "emotional atmosphere" of this pre-MidPoint stage. Logically, there can only be disorder before order, irrationality before rationality, ignorance before knowledge.

As thinking beings we need to be rational and objective, but related to Evolution within our reality. Our feelings need to be balanced, natural, out of conflict. This education of human feelings will be better achieved if the conflicting turmoil of opposites is eliminated so that we can feel security in our link with Evolution.

This is the great paradox, which some have called the human tragedy. But this dense fog of gross ignorance is about to lift. The top, most knowledgeable leaders are clearing the fog. They cannot wait for the omnipotent wave of a wand by an imagined god. Even if there were such a deity, would it not give help to those who are already helping themselves rather than those who neglect to seize their responsibility when it is necessary?

People must be put in the picture as it really is. Superstition must now be overcome so that the second phase of human Evolution can proceed without all the fiery turmoil of self-destruction. We must face up to reality which is more wonderful and delightful and exciting than this world can dream of in its present condition.

The Big Question Remains: "Does God Exist?"
The sociological dilemma: how we prove that God exists, remains unanswered, uncertain and unproven except to the most faithful believers.

If we can accept that God does exist – just for a moment - Does God have a gender, a race, a material colour? Is he or she to be loved or feared? Soft, subjective questions to answer. People who believe in God, believe. People who disbelieve in God, disbelieve. Those who don't know, don't know. Which one is right?

It is not controversial then to say that even in this twenty-first century we still cannot be sure that God exists but we can be sure that Evolution exists: the great ongoing power or life force, the energy that is behind all that is, both visible to us as humans as well as invisible. Sociologists, psychiatrists, metaphysicians, theological researchers, all experts in social evolution continue to debate if, and how, divine intervention has provided the templates for Evolution. It is an endlessly fascinating and awe-inspiring subject.

Theologian Sarah Coakley, Professor of Divinity at Cambridge University and Canon at Ely Cathedral, takes a Natural Theology perspective, posing the question:

"Is the evolutionary narrative one of pure randomness and essential meaninglessness or do the patterns of mankind's cooperation, mutation and selection suggest a picture in which teleology (ie the doctrine of design and purpose in the material world) holds some meaning? Contemporary debates about the purpose of evolutionary cooperation therefore represent a fork in the road between different unitary readings of evolution's meaning. Does evolution bespeak nothing but competitive 'genetic selfishness' or is there some alternative that might itself enhance the expansion of human altruism to face the pressing contemporary political, ethical and ecological crises we face?"(Sarah Coakley, talk to Ely Cathedral, 2017)

We must here acknowledge polytheism: that different gods from different mythological and religious backgrounds are worshipped for different purposes. However, conflicts between both major and minor religious movements throughout history have been divisive and dysfunctional to our world. Had those religious leaders and their supporters understood that the Law of Evolution, or Natural Theology as it may also be called, has shaped its divine imprint on the structure of life in all its forms, then humankind could find much common spiritual ground to share for the greater benefit of all.

A third dilemma, both a metaphysical and spiritual one: as yet there is no scientific evidence to define or describe life after death, despite its existence being the foundation stone of all the world religions.

The essential truth is that humankind is not just a mortal creature of earthly ways, we are spiritual creatures conceived and precipitated into physical form in order that the Intelligence, or Evolution, can realise its creation. All religious movements agree the concept of eternal life and some believe in an infinite goal of perfect transcendental bliss, an awareness that knowledge of this brings everlasting life to man as the spirit has no limitations in time or space. Therefore, the life of the person after earthly discontinuance is still the life of the Intelligence moving towards ultimate realisation of the original conception. Whilst the physical body deteriorates, the spirit cannot. Our fear of death is often a frantic concern for self and fear of the unknown. Man may not perceive himself as part of the continuum of eternity stretching thousands of years before his birth and existing thousands of years after his death. For such a person, with limited vision, there is only birth and death.

To quote the words of the renowned Maharishi Mahesh Yogi, *"If the human mind aligns itself with all the laws of nature at their source, understanding there is a unified field, such a mind gains the support of natural law. Every thought and action would then be supported by the infinite intelligence displayed throughout the universe."*

How, though, can we achieve such higher mental states, a spiritual enlightenment, when our minds are full of earthly matters? Only by searching for what does not make sense can we examine the Philosophy of the Unconscious and by being aware enough to admit that if we have not found a falsehood in our thinking and feeling, we have found a truth. Each person must find his or her own spiritual consciousness in order to see the truth.

What is Man's Place in Evolution?

The evolutionary force permeating the universe consists of millions of solar systems in infinity, dimensionless, timeless, immeasurable. Greater minds than mine have asked why humankind, so intrinsically a part of the evolutionary process, remains so divided, polarised and perpetually conflicted even to the point of potentially hastening its own extinction? What would it take to harvest the great knowledge and insights born of man's inquisitiveness and intellect and to combine them with a transcendental spiritual understanding which would escalate humankind's experience, and achieve higher level cooperation with other living species, for the greater benefit of this generation, and all those in the future?

In *The Sane Society*, eminent social psychologist and humanistic philosopher Erich Fromm, proposed:

"Man first emerged from the animal world as a freak of nature. Having lost most of the instinctive equipment which regulate animals' activities, he was more helpless, less well equipped for the fight for survival than most animals yet he developed the capacity for thought, imagination and self-awareness, which was the basis for transforming nature and himself. He severed the tie with nature and with mother Earth and set himself a new goal, that of being fully born, of being fully awake, of being fully human, of being free. Yet today, when man seems to have reached the beginning of a new, richer, happier human era, his existence, and that of generations to follow, is more threatened than ever. Man has won his freedom from clerical and secular authorities, standing alone with his reason and his conscience as his only judges, but is afraid of the newly won freedom. He has achieved the 'freedom from' without having achieved the 'freedom to': to be himself, to be fully productive, to be fully awake. To put it differently, the aim of modern man was to create a sane society, whose members have developed objective reason, permitting them to see themselves, others, nature in their true reality not distorted by infantile omniscience or paranoid hate. So far, we have failed."

Uncovering underlying spiritual truths means clearing away all rituals, superstitions, mystical notions, which all act like gossip to the enlightenment of the mind. We tend to divide every aspect of life into opposites. We talk of light and dark, for example, as though there were two different states, two different experiences and polarise our experiences in every field of our lives: politics, religion, fraternity, education and so on.

Evolution follows a relentless, unwavering course, unaltered significantly by humankind despite its wish for omnipotence. It is a process of organised, ever-adapting creative development with all energy and intelligence contained within the process itself. It is the most meticulously perfect system that ever existed. It is the blueprint for life because it is life; it is what life is. We humans are the perpetual defaulters and blame everyone and everything, even blind superstition for our sad and painful misfortunes. The real truth, the absolute truth, is that there is no blame to be apportioned. It is part of the programme of Evolution that humankind's development takes place stage by stage.

Evolution works on the basis of perfect equilibrium, inter-coordination, and progressive movement. It is all controlled by a built-in self-adjusting mechanism which regulates the on-going creative plan. Evolution is ever-adapting to the changing circumstances within itself to sustain its equilibrium – a key requirement in all of creation.

Chapter 1: Evolution, The Intelligence and Our Unconscious

Evolution has no independent agenda. There is nothing personal about its performance. It has one sole objective, to pursue perpetual self-adjustment, its innate blueprint for its achievement. At the most macro level we see this if a person cuts part of the body, say a finger: the bleeding will stop by natural means, dead and damaged cells will be removed from the site of the damage, new cells will be created. The damaged flesh will slowly build up, cell by cell towards the surface, and finally the finger will be restored to its rightful design. Quite remarkable and yet so commonplace. Are we not all in awe of the wonder of nature, of Evolution? Are we not glad we are part of the same incredible scheme?

The same dynamic mechanisms used in the whole evolutionary process operate within each living creature, not just humans, making some able to adjust perfectly to their environment, in others bringing about all the changes needed. It is an iterative self-adjusting creativity. Humankind needs only to observe and perform in this stage of cosmic development.

Evolution will *always* dynamically strive for restoration of equilibrium once it has been lost. Immediately, it makes appropriate adjustments, modifications, changes. There is perpetual adaptation, it is Evolution's way. It makes its own way, so to say, directed by its own genius. Such genius could equally be applied to advanced humans when their creative and purposeful direction is determined. Evolution knows where it is going: the growth and diversification of species in its own time. We will all fulfil ourselves and ripen, like the cherry on the tree.

Nevertheless, the facilities for redressing balance, restoring order and maintaining equilibrium are available to each individual, dependent on their conceptual learning on the route from ignorance to knowledge. When an error in our progress is discerned, we may realise it, and maximise that learning moment, moving forwards as fully and efficiently as we are capable of. However, failing to observe our error is all too common and is both an individual and a societal loss which slows the speed of personal and communal progress. This is the price of our own built-in self-adjustment device.

Man's creativity is unlimited. There is no point at which he will say he cannot improve on this, rectify that, moderate something else, learn more, improve himself. There is always a margin for further growth and few limits to the supply of energy for this creativeness.

The key limitation to man's creativity is that caused by irrational thinking which becomes repressed eg too much fantasy, false beliefs, prejudices, doubts, fears, guilts and other factors causing sensory confusion. The very nature of the unconscious is largely incomprehensible to Western populations because they have limited and selected knowledge, little of which is concerned with abstract and spiritual values. Self-directed subservience to the unconscious does mean that the consciousness of this individual will change. Important present goals may later become seen as corrupted thinking.

That Evolution has a universal unconscious plan is clear to me, and the aim of this writing is to dispel doubts that may exist in the reader's mind, to whom I hope to offer a philosophy that glimpses the answer to many of mankind's unsolved mysteries. The unconscious, Evolution, has a philosophy complete unto itself. There is no judgement upon itself. There is no conception of error or imperfection. The human errors of confusion and corruption discussed in this work can be traced to secondary factors, and not the primary one. When these errors are removed or corrected through enlightenment, man is restored to creative living with purity and peace.

We could ask if it would not have been easier if such a supreme intelligence had been intelligent enough to allow mortals to know what their destiny was intended to be? Perhaps it is part of the conceived plan that man shall find his own philosophy by the usual method of trial and error?

That the conscious mind is concerned with measurement, judgement, correcting imperfections and is able to change at any time through changing environmental circumstances means it can provide its own pleasure, through the satisfaction of achievement. The conscious mind has so much to do to improve its individual's experience, it cannot achieve it alone. It is most helpful that the

Intelligence, operating through the unconscious, is not concerned with the physical factors individuals encounter in their environment, but only with the systematic fulfilment of the conceived plan, or blueprint. The unconscious has no margin for adapting for it is perfection. The plan still goes on. All the forces of perfection are there to be utilised to ensure perfect harmony. Spiritual harmony is always within regardless of what is happening without. What we name as being happy, peaceful, relaxed, successful, creative, emotionally literate are the outcomes of perfect creativity which existed long before language was created to name them.

Individuals today have the same opportunities to be perfectly directed as anyone from any past civilisations. The factors which prevail in our earthly existence were not, and are not, consequential or instrumental in the creativeness of the Intelligence, as it is internal and not externally manifested. We should understand things not as the world presents them with earthly values but as the Intelligence supplies them, through the spirit. With voluntary subservience to the Intelligence, all selfishness and conceit falls away from mental life: the self ceases to matter, only affection for the Intelligence remains.

Evolution designed and created a broad variety of species of humankind, one of which was homo sapiens, who embraces the spiritual sphere, an element of life of which we are inextricably a part. In order to know ourselves and to direct relations with

the Intelligence, humankind must first understand the
emotional defences that blind us to the reality of
ourselves and our environment, which paralyse such
enlightenment.

Physical life becomes the mere experience and
expression of spiritual life, for which there is no birth,
death, youth, age, disease. The heart and soul can be
free from false notions of mortal, sensory confusion.
When one is freed from these fallacies one becomes a
truly dynamic creative being. Each person is perfect
health, and creatively pure.

The chaos of the pre-MidPoint is an inevitable
phenomenon. It will be so until knowledge is collated
skilfully. <u>That is the foundation of the MidPoint stage</u>:
the collation of knowledge, the consequent reduction
of ignorance, and the drawing up of man's blueprint
for his future. Our destiny demands it. Our life
physically depends on it, because without the
workshop of physical existence the soul of man
cannot survive. The spiritual is contained in the
physical - it can only manifest itself and flourish in
the cut-and-thrust of life, in the conflicting
experiences from which grains of truth can be
assimilated – the essences of life as they become
understood in the pursuit of knowledge of the soul.

Construction starts to replace destruction in the
New Age, its philosophy rejecting naturalistic and
materialistic philosophies because such explanations
deny any sacred dimension. The seismograph is
already detecting the initial tremors of what is to be.

The leaders of the New Age proposed to teach us to know ourselves and help us to release our creative potential to its fullest in the Evolutionary system of which we are all an essential part. Love of life and self and others will become the rightful emotion for the New Age civilisation, possible, <u>now</u>, for the first time as we move beyond the stage of hate and violence experienced during the pre-MidPoint stage.

As the spiritual aspects of life lead to higher consciousness and an inner truth, we should view all reality from this perspective. The romantic philosopher poets of the 1800s: Emerson, Whitman, Thoreau, rejected the God of the Bible, instead writing at length about a transcendent quality of spirituality experienced purely through personal introspection. These ideas gained popular momentum here in the West during the 1960s and 70s when high profile musical celebrities' involvement with transcendental meditation awakened a generation's interests in honing their personal contract with God rather than in formalised mass ritual: Buddhism, Scientology, meditation and other spiritual practices benefitted.

This new perspective of personal attainment provides a vital inspiration. It is all the same reality of which mankind is part, always has been and probably always will be. However, without an internal perspective and self-identification we remain in the darkest of places.

There is only order. There is only harmony. There is only truth. There is only beauty. There is only one meticulously creative programme of which we are all a part. The basic laws of connection which direct and manifest our individual creations in terms of gifts, talents, potentialities are just not understood although there is sufficient knowledge available in the numerous educational and spiritual disciplines to form an integrated picture, and so the blue print for human living can now be formulated to become a basic structure established for the whole of society.

Of course, we must conquer our stubbornness, waywardness, and vindictiveness. We must find a measure of humility. We must be prepared to learn quickly, perhaps intuitively, and change direction quickly. No more procrastination.

There is a challenge to be taken. Now, the MidPoint stage is upon us all. The pre-MidPoint merges into the MidPoint, the embryo breaks through the shell and embarks on the new role of fledgling.

Is this New Age enlightenment so hard to grasp? Our politicians have held many philosophies and values, but what a disparate range of political movements have been imposed on our societies to achieve some "civilising" standards?

We have a tendency to want more and more information before committing ourselves when, in reality, we probably are sufficiently informed. While some may be driven to find greater truths, different knowledge, an enhanced reputation or greater glory, when we come together to put the pieces together, like a giant jigsaw puzzle, not separately but jointly and creatively in acknowledgement of the continuing development of our whole civilisation, each discipline benefits from greater knowledge, imagination, wisdom. Shouldn't our aim be to support the evolutionary process in order to benefit ourselves, our society and future generations, by our enhancement in the physical order of things, its harmony and its equilibrium? What are our barriers? Do we seek to become divine ourselves?

We live in extraordinary times. We have knowledge of spiritual, metaphysical, psychological matters but have not yet found a way to transform these into a single beneficial philosophy for living.

It is important to realise just how much the concepts of "sin" and "godliness" have been embedded in our souls and how suffused by the concepts of God and the Devil, good and evil. Only now – at the arrival of the New Age – can these opposites be understood once and for all. It all implies that man has failed as a socialised group because we have not achieved perfection or Godliness in our collective behaviour. We are sinners. Religion has supported this view to blackmail the fearful into choosing God's commandments. All civilisations so far have based their philosophies on this powerful message – and still do.

Historically, mankind has sought divine intervention to define and give credibility to its behaviours, resulting in many world religions, largely in pursuit of a serene after-life. Yet western enlightenment sustains an expectation that people should take personal responsibility for their lives and those of their families. Many of the world religions have dwindling support today whilst there is greater excitement that science can extend our lives, expand our consciousness, even create a new biomedical model of "human". Our greatest thinkers have, between them, sufficient knowledge for this stage of man's continued development on planet Earth. This is humankind's ultimate objective – and now is the time!

In his contemporary assessment of the extent of religions' controls, *Homo Deus*, visionary historian YN Harari contemplates: *"Human cooperatives and networks usually judge themselves by yardsticks of their own invention and, unsurprisingly, often give themselves high marks. Those built in the name of imaginary entities usually judge success from that imaginary viewpoint."*

Now at the MidPoint we must move beyond endless discussions and theorising about the whys and whats just to satisfy our curiosity in order to understand as much as can be understood about the dynamics of all life's functions. All such dynamic human endeavour must be directed to the New Age cause, and the focussing of the periphery on to the centre.

The great law of Evolution is this: It is impossible for man to make a mistake. Evolution will not perpetuate its "mistakes".

Much debate has taken place about whether, and how, our society needs to make urgent adjustments, even radical changes, to achieve a relatively stable society, and because many changes are required in almost every department of our lives.

It may be quite impossible for one book to provide sufficient comment to address all the issues. It is, however, my purpose, to be one small part of the New Age groundswell embracing the expanding boundaries of knowledge that contemporary scientists and technologists are discovering at this cusp of the old Millennium and beginning of the new.

Such an enormity of knowledge is overwhelming but is essential for imagination to take its rightful place in this new synthesis. There is, of course, not one single problem to be resolved but a multiplicity of them, of great complexity, which challenge our civilisation and our social boundaries, which are exercising some of our greatest minds, across a range of disciplines at this very time.

My own belief is that the main reason for this rise in conflict is a lack of insight into the "unity of opposites". I hope to show how the chaotic disorders which have caused a crisis in our civilisation are due to natural Evolutionary developments; unavoidable, as social standards, values and principles change. It is humankind who has a confused understanding about its place.

Chapter 2
The Psychology of Man's Development

In the mid twentieth century, a drastic change began, a change as great as ever occurred in the past. New techniques replaced the use of physical energy of animals and men by that of steam, oil, electricity, creating means of communication which transformed the earth into the size of one continent, and the human race into one society, where the fate of one is the fate of all. They created productive forces which permit everybody to have a dignified material existence, and reduced work to such dimensions that it filled only a fraction of a man's day. Modern humanity has been alienated from the world of its own creation. Man has become part of the machine, experiencing himself as commodity, alienating himself in his aim to sell himself profitably on the market, his value as a person lying in his saleability not his human qualities of love and reason, or his artistic capabilities. What is the alternative? The only alternative to the danger of roboticism is humanistic communitarianism: creating a community of work, to share experiences, to prevent the profit motive from directing production into socially harmful directions. Man must be restituted to his supreme place in society.

Erich Fromm, *The Sane Society*, 1955

The Philosophy of the Unconscious may be difficult to understand but, as we can all gain more when re-reading information for a second or third time, so with repeated contemplation and meditation, leaning away from the physical to the spiritual, we can gain more insight into the reality of the Intelligence.

The world of the Intelligence, permeating the universe of millions of solar systems, is infinite.

It is acknowledged by all religions that man is influenced by inner strivings, probably from before his birth, but he constantly needs to readjust to this environment as his life evolves. Our reason for being here on Earth, and for progressing step by step and stage by stage, is to learn and learn more. The Intelligence has variously been described as the Holy Ghost, communion with nature, or destiny. However we perceive it, the person may find the first intimation of the spirit as a revelation and whether he is fulfilled the same day or at a later time, this is the understanding through which we understand the principle of revelation, until we reach perfection.

We see proof of this all the time, in the dynamic curiosity of any young child: their desire to know why. Who can doubt it? In this way they gather experiences, remember past happenings, attempt to satisfy their strivings and desires. If they use their powers of thinking rationally they will be able to make their own adjustments to assist their own progress, however irrational their inner urges are.

Now consider this principle: spiritual movements believe that humankind is just one part of a multifaceted universe. Can we then argue that Evolution is not that powerful driver?

Once we begin to understand the life we are living, and realise that we are inevitably and inextricably interacting with it all the time, then human imagination and consciousness becomes focused to the point of action where it should be: to be alert, keen, willing to understand, then our innate curiosity will have no bounds. There is no limit to the creative powers of Evolution, or the creative powers of the individual.

After years of dissatisfaction with computer models of the brain, a debate on the nature of "mind" escalated in 1987 with the publication of *The Theory of Mind*, when Nobel laureate Gerald Edelman attempted to explain the workings of the mind in terms of Darwinian selection. It was a long, complex argument (*Ed note: which few neurologists had commented on during the 1990s when this author was researching*). Edelman set out his theory that perception, action and learning are preserved and their connections become strengthened. Those that do not are eliminated, by a self-correcting process of adaption which continues throughout life. Memories rather than being stored in neat compartments are continually reworked and recategorised by every life experience, from before birth until death, continuously altering and shaping our brains. (Gerald

Edelman, *Neural Darwinism: The Theory of Neuronal Group Selection,* 1987).

But what happens if the on-going soul of the person does not learn, continues to make the same error, refuses to recognise it, has a preconceived bias or prejudice, or believes that it did not happen, or blames someone else for their error? It means the opportunity for learning a valuable lesson has been missed. This is a failing to understand the basic point of the Law of Trial and Error and prevents us from attaining the fundamental desire to fulfil ourselves, to be the best we can be.

Individuals repeatedly make recordings through their five physical senses and apply reasons as best they can to their findings, often against difficult obstacles and conditions, often not understanding exactly what is happening, endeavouring to bring greater harmony within themselves and to make greater personal progress in day-to-day affairs.

The forces that motivate us are essentially unconscious. However, the conscious mind receives impressions from birth, perhaps from the time of conception, and those impressions influence the unconscious: sometimes aiding our instincts, sometimes restricting them.

Readjustment is a difficult process needing rational guidance. Throughout this process, some satisfactions will need to be postponed, some restricted, some consciously repressed temporarily or permanently, and so on. There will be a pattern of self-gain and self-deprivation according to man's idea of self: the Ego-ideal.

Briefly summarising, there are five urges at work in our Unconscious: i) rational predestined instincts with their appropriate end aims; ii) irrational fantasies; iii) misrouted instincts; iv) repressed instincts surging for re-expression and v) superego forces providing some form of punishment. All except the first are produced as a result of environmental influences which shape man's growth and progress. They occur later in development than the instincts present at birth, even before birth, even before the first cell of the embryo.

Given their free and uncontaminated expression, our primary instincts would lead to perfect harmony, growth and fulfilment because this is the blueprint held by the primary intelligence, the Philosophy of the Unconscious. However, instinctive urges influenced by external stimuli can lose their direction, become misdirected causing anxiety, tension, leading to mental and physical disorders in a cyclical way, creating a vicious circle of tension and fear.

Before the theory that unconscious forces of humankind are all predestined to bring about its harmonious and creative development can be fully understood, it is necessary to examine with care, within the scope of this work, some other mental forces which also become unconscious and produce disorganisation and corruption. It is hard to believe that the forces are essentially pure when the behaviour is often corrupt. I hope to show that such counter-forces, secondary influences, arise from environmental stimuli and that it is flawed reality thinking which causes a faulty reaction to the stimuli and, in turn, brings subsequent errors. This is why misconceptions come about.

Consider these statements by two ordinary human beings: colleague Dr Leslie Weatherhead finds "life is a wonderful creative adventure abounding with happiness and success" whilst past patient Mr ALG said "Life is like hell on earth." Which one is right? Can they both be right? Are they both wrong?

It will be shown that the Philosophy of the Unconscious is "peace, happiness and success". All else is mortal corruption. But first we must examine other emotional factors of the Unconscious. The two most powerful emotional factors that play a great part in our lives are hatred and love.

Hatred of self, or others, is an emotional reaction to frustration. Children can be heard to shout "I hate you!" when they cannot have their own way. It is not an original instinctive drive. When a child behaves in an aggressive way, it is an environmental reaction; the child has not yet learned the difference between what is expected and what is not. The aim of aggression – itself a reaction to fear – is only a striving for the end of an uncomfortable situation, it is not usually a demonstration of pleasure in destruction. I am emphatic about this point in matters of child delinquency and criminology generally. Hatred can come from a feeling of fear. Sibling rivalry arises from unconscious resentments, manifesting in jealousy. Hate is a result of frustration and fear produced by environmental stimuli and is not part of natural law. Fear will also bring tension to the nervous and muscular systems of the body and this tension is often sufficient to produce symptoms which will force their way back into consciousness. It is a fear of having a fear.

These instincts often become severely disorganised. In order to break the vicious circle, somehow, somewhere, an instinct will have to be redirected towards its intended aim. Redirection and reassurance must take place before equilibrium can be achieved. Beneath the vicious circle of frantic confusion the forces of inner restoration are still available to bring clear-sightedness, rationality, relaxation and confidence. These instincts are still striving for harmony and growth. When there is no further corruption the plan proceeds systematically and the end-aim of mature creativity will develop.

Because of the ambivalent nature of these emotions in childhood, love is seldom present with elements of hate. The less hatred there is, the purer and more ego-releasing the emotion of love will be when love is experienced. Hatred is a force of contamination and corruption created by circumstances of the environment but it must be understood that the individual is not always responsible for the fear experience. If hatred is experienced and repressed into the Unconscious it can be released by later readjustment, maturity and insight.

Love that is relatively free from ambivalence is compatible. This more mature form of love is combined with reality rather than fantasy thinking but it must be based on realistic knowledge of the object of that love. If an individual is able to grasp and interpret the outside world realistically with realistic ego-ideal, or self-valuation, hatred of self and others will be minimal and be free from the complications of subjective distortions.

However, some people's early sexual experiences may be associated with specific, difficult memories. If shyness inhibits a man when experiencing his first sexual relationship he could feel like a failure. If a woman has fears, tenses up in the love-relationship it could cause her pain and no pleasure. Such negative early associations dramatically and seriously interfere with natural evolutionary drives and responses. Natural spontaneous enjoyment and fulfilment might well be impossible, instigating emotions of frustration, disappointment, all distinctly negative emotions about fears of failure, of impotence, of ineffectiveness, and the disillusionment, the shame, the fault, the arguments, the anger. These are some of the emotions that arise and work against the natural laws of Evolution.

Throughout this research both rational and irrational forces affecting human behaviour have been examined. Behaviour is usually called rational if it is based on intelligent observation of the facts available together with intelligent assessment and insight into the true situation so that logically appropriate action can be taken to achieve a desirable end.

It is called irrational if observations of fact are false and if reasoning is incorrect or inappropriate.

The pattern of human life consists of certain individual behaviours relating to other members of their kind, expressing collectively the instinctive strivings for a desirable end-aim. If confused or conflicting urges arise from the Unconscious, perhaps based on fantasy thinking, or mis-routed striving, or an adverse intent, that person's behaviour will become irrational. Strivings are entirely rational if they are directed purposefully from the Unconscious in harmony with the end of the instinct involved.

But, what self-confidence can be achieved if a person believes, when he makes an error, that he has failed? Typically, a sense of defeat, a sense of not being able enough, not trying hard enough. If the mistake seems momentous, maybe the erring person will blame others, or life, or society, or even their God for their predicament. In fact, it only means that they did not know themselves well enough. The reality is more likely to be their lack of awareness of the breadth of the problem, a shortage of knowledge to achieve a good result. It is notable that in societies where populations have knowledge deliberately withheld from them, where self-direction is skewed, their misunderstandings will be more frequent and their responses to them inappropriate. This will be distressing for them.

Trial and Error
The basic laws of creation which direct and manifest our individual creativeness in terms of gifts, talents, abilities, sensitivities – our inner potentialities, are just not understood, and that is the prime cause of the existing circumstances at the pre-MidPoint stage. Although, the great paradox is this: there is sufficient knowledge available at the present time, which can be gleaned from all the advanced disciplines in the world to form an integrated picture of the greater reality of Evolution and to establish the blue-print for the MidPoint stage – the New Age. It is a joint recapitulation of all advanced knowledge that is required at the MidPoint.

Ordinary people need to have a structure for living, and if the facts and laws are not clearly defined and revealed they will continue to move ahead with uncertainty and insecurity. Too many haphazard trials, insufficiently thought-out concepts, and too many errors are being made, characteristic of the pre-MidPoint stage. They can only cause delay in progress, disappointment and frustration – especially if the process continues interminably.

At the pre-MidPoint stage there is always cockiness and irrational behaviour. These are all too prevalent immature emotions that break surface and disrupt. It is inevitable at such a stage in any growing civilisation where there is too much ignorance and therefore insufficient enlightenment. Children will say, in a cocky manner, "I know best!" or words to that effect, and it is inevitable at that early stage of growing up. Some humans never advance beyond that stage in their own infantile development, let alone when airing their views later in society. It is all so logical and utterly rational, as knowledge comes slowly and ignorance dies only by the same degree. But we must come to understand that Evolution knows best. We cannot go on being arrogant, self-opinionated and aggressive in our inter-human relationships forever. We are at the pre-MidPoint stage and actually <u>have</u> sufficient knowledge available before us – here and <u>now</u> – if we can get our blinkers off and if necessary put on a pair of spectacles that will give us a better focus on the greater reality.

The truth is, we are actually learning all the time, but have not been knowledgeable of the ways of Evolution, keenly looking for the tell-tale, illuminating error that sends us on our way with ever-growing understanding and self-confidence.

What self-confidence is there if a person believes, when he makes an error, that he has failed? Unfortunately, a vast number of humans do believe this irrational and depressing fact. It only means that they do not know themselves well enough at the present moment.

Errors are magical moments, essentially part of the learning process, for that is the psychological moment of added knowledge. But what happens if the on-going soul of the person does not learn, continues to make the same error, refuses to recognise it, has a preconceived bias or prejudice, or believes that it did not happen, or blames someone else for the error? It means the opportunity for learning a valuable lesson has been missed. This is the prime reason why full understanding of the Law of Trial and Error must be understood – and actually used by all humans who are, after all, wishing to gradually fulfil themselves according to the natural law. The law has been noticed and talked about for decades, but never used as one of the tools of life.

This is one of the many essential laws of creation that have been almost entirely ignored. Everyone wants to believe that they do not make errors. But only because they do not understand the creative nature of them.

It is still surprising how, if some momentous mistake does take place, the erring person will blame others, or life, or society, or even God for the ghastly predicament experienced. The only problem, if one can call it such, is lack of sufficient knowledge to achieve the satisfactory result. It is true, however, that in a society where insufficient knowledge is available, where there is no programme of self-direction, errors become more frequent and distressing. Unless – we understand the law and live by it. There are many such laws and we humans must live by them all. What are they there for otherwise? Is Evolution a product of a blundering chaos, or are our own minds at fault?

Man's creativity is potentially unlimited. There is no point at which he will say he cannot improve on this, rectify that, moderate something else, learn more, improve himself. There is always a margin for further growth and few limits to the supply of energy for this creativeness.

However, one limitation to man's creativity is that caused by irrational thinking which becomes repressed eg too much fantasy, false beliefs, prejudices, doubts, fears, guilts and other factors causing sensory confusion. The very nature of the Unconscious is largely incomprehensible to Western populations because individuals have limited and selected knowledge, little of which is concerned with abstract and spiritual values.

Evolution has a built-in self-adjusting mechanism which regulates the on-going creative plan. There is perpetual self-adjustment to the environment, and the facilities for redressing balance, restoring order and maintaining equilibrium are available to the individual as well. This is based on his conceptual learning on the route from ignorance to knowledge: when an error in our progress is discerned, and we maximise on that learning moment, we have moved forwards as fully and efficiently as we can. Failing to observe the error is a great loss of opportunity, and can only result in reduction of speed of personal progress. This is part of our own built-in self-adjustment device.

The reason for being here on Earth, and for progressing step by step and stage by stage, is to learn and learn. Why do you think a young child is charged with the dynamic power of curiosity?

If we once begin to understand the life we are living, and realise that we are inevitably and inextricably interacting with it all the time, then human imagination and consciousness will become focused to the point of action where it should be. Then we will all become alert, keen and sharp and our innate curiosity will have no bounds. There is no limit to the creative powers of Evolution, or the creative powers of the individual, a soul, a spark, an off-shoot from the whole enormous scheme of all that is. Individuals learn from their errors – of behaviour and outlook and judgement – and so do civilisations which are mass individuals. Get the foundations firmly in place, and then start to build.

Humans are social creatures who seek a group to belong to and a structure for living to adhere to, and if the facts and laws of their society are not clearly defined and revealed they will function in uncertainty and insecurity. All religions concede that man is influenced by his inner strivings, maybe from before his birth, and constantly needs to readjust to his environment as his life evolves. In this way he gathers experiences, remembers past happenings, attempts to satisfy his strivings, desires and interests. If he uses his powers of thinking rationally he will be able to make his own adjustments to assist his progress, however irrational his inner urges are.

At this stage, something must be written concerning emotional direction of the self, the way by which Intelligence achieves its aim. The instincts are essentially emotions, causing motions of the mind and needing to have an object at which to direct its discharge. The curiosity instinct, for example, must have something about which to become curious. The combat instinct must have a reason to combat. The repulsion instinct must have an object to recoil from, and so on. This object may either be the individual him or herself or an external object within the environment.

When a baby is born it is, at first, aware only of its physical self: toes, fingers, tactile sensations. Its instincts are entirely self-directed, its curiosity entirely ego-centric. The ego-centricity of the instinctive urges of infancy is essential for it to discover itself before it begins to discover the world of non-self, to discover its relationship to its environment. Maturity depends on the flow of instinctive energy through the medium of material forms, outwards towards objects in the environment. Only when the curiosity instinct is directed to subjects, things and people outside of itself, can our ego develop rationally. If our curiosity were to remain ego-centric we would remain in an emotional state of isolation. Emotional development, then, consists of a maturing process from the infantile state of self-concern and indifference to the non-self, to a state where concern relates primarily to the non-self.

Why does it prove so impossible for our civilisation to celebrate the rich diversity of knowledge across its cultures and generations? Astounding universal benefits would accrue from sharing the knowledge, insights and altruistic ambitions of our greatest minds, in every area of learning.

Sir Julian Huxley, humanist and one of the twentieth century's leading exponents of evolutionary theory, called for a radical rethinking of Western social structures through education:

"The world has become one, de facto. It must therefore achieve some unification of thought if it is to avoid disaster and this can only come about with the aid of education. We must remember that two-fifths of the world's adult population is still illiterate, that the world's provision for education at all levels is lamentably inadequate, and that under-developed countries are clamouring for more and better education. Make no mistake, the basic task before the educational profession today is to study and understand the evolutionary humanist revolution, in all its ramifications, to follow up its educational implication, and

to enable as many as possible of the world's growing minds to be illuminated by its new view of human destiny." (Julian Huxley, *Towards a New Humanism*, 1957.)

However, we know that no educational revolution took place and material improvements in our lifestyles have clearly not created happier experiences generally. Paradoxically, in Peru, Guatemala, the Philippines and Albania, all countries suffering poverty and political instability, one person in 100,000 commits suicide each year. In rich and peaceful countries: France, Japan, Switzerland and New Zealand it is 25 people per 100,000. More, recent studies have shown in the USA that wellbeing levels in the 1990s were much the same as they were in the depressed 1950s. That aspirational pinnacle we call Happiness is held tantalisingly aloft by two different pillars: one psychological and one biological.

How then may we capitalise on the wisdoms of our combined philosophies for future generations? Erich Fromm reflected:

"The politics of the West and East both rest on nineteenth century ideals. The West in the name of the ideas of the French revolution: on liberty, on reason, on individualism. In the East, on the name of socialist ideas of solidarity and equality. They both succeed in capturing the imagination and fanatical allegiance of hundreds of millions of people. Today there is a decisive difference between the two systems. In the Western world, there is

freedom to express ideas critical of the existing system. In the East, criticism and expression of different ideas is suppressed by brutal force. The former carries within itself the possibility for peaceful progressive transformation whilst for the latter, such possibilities are almost non-existent. However, both are based on industrialisation, ever increasing economic growth. It is to be assumed that the more the East develops economically the less severely it will exploit the majority of the population. The West develops rapidly in the direction of Huxley's Brave New World, today the East is Orwell's 1984 – but both systems tend to converge, are becoming managerial societies, their inhabitants well fed, well clad, their wishes satisfied they become automatons, following without being forced, guided without leadership, making machines which act like man and men who act like machines, whose reason deteriorates while their intelligence rises, creating the dangerous situation of equipping man with the greatest material power without the wisdom to use it. Our dangers are war and robotism. In the nineteenth century the problem was that God was dead. In the twentieth it is that Man is dead. In the nineteenth century inhumanity meant cruelty, in the twentieth it means schizoid self-alienation. The danger of the past is that men became slaves. The danger of the future is that men may become robots and while they may not rebel, they cannot live and remain sane, and will destroy their world because they cannot stand any longer the boredom of a meaningless life." (Erich Fromm, *The Sane Society*, 1955)

Contemporary Israeli philosopher, YH Harari, in *Homo Deus: A Brief History of Tomorrow*, warns us very specifically, analysing how technology will destroy humankind's future if we don't act fast. He warns us of the dangers of sleepwalking into giving up our control to the world's software engineers solely because the rate of technological change today is so fast.

"What shall we strive for: immortality, happiness, divinity? Failure to adapt to the fast pace of technological change could have some terrifying consequences. Silicon Valley will have only the social visions their engineers can produce. Man's quest for immortality will lead us to upgrade ourselves biologically. Our belief in the possibility of an eternal soul could lead us to destroy humanity as we know it. Nano robots may search our blood for pathogens to destroy, human brains may be connected to the internet able to call on a wealth of knowledge simply by thinking about it. Our brains could be connected to one another: an internet of minds. The possibility of great inequality is built into all this. Biological upgrades will not be shared equally, potentially creating a cognitive elite that will view the rest of mankind with the same superiority that Sapiens once reserved for Neanderthals. It's not something that will happen in thousands of years, it is a timescale of decades. In a world where almost all jobs are automated, the elites will have little use for the masses and huge job losses will occur. As the working classes are becoming a non-working class and perhaps the first part of a 'useless' class, so the next

wave of change will be brought about by Artificial Intelligence and will threaten the middle classes because these are jobs that are also easy to automate. What made us Sapiens will make us gods. We had better think carefully otherwise we may gain victory in old battlefields only to be caught unawares on new fronts in the twenty first century. If science is right and our happiness is determined by our biochemical system, then the only way to get everlasting happiness is by manipulating human biochemistry. This is exactly what we have been doing with psychiatric drugs over the last few decades but are we not misguided to regard individual happiness as the highest form of human society? Homo sapiens was not adapted by evolution to experience constant pleasure but if that is what humankind wants, it will be necessary to change our biochemistry and re-engineer our minds and bodies.

Where are the leaders offering a different vision? One central project will be to protect mankind from the dangers inherent in our own power. Though we have managed to bring famine, plague and war under control thanks largely to our phenomenal economic growth which provides us with abundant food, medicine, energy and raw materials, this same growth destabilises the equilibrium of the planet in myriad ways which we have only just begun to explore."

Historically, education has aimed to fill the lower mind, organising our memories to absorb facts, synthesising history and achievements, repeating the lessons learned so far: the basic measurement of our previous enquiries as human beings, both individually and collectively.

The objective of New Age Education is different. It prepares us for the next stage in the cognitive development of our humanity and harnesses the understandings which arise. All activities which drive humans forward, be they physical, mental, emotional, social or institutional, so long as they advance our present state, are essentially spiritual in nature and indicative of the presence of a divine entity within us.

"A cultural renaissance must combine with education for the young, for adult education, and a new system of popular art and secular ritual throughout our nations. Man can protect himself from the consequences of his own madness only by creating a sane society, which conforms with the needs of man, which is rooted in the bonds of brotherliness and solidarity rather than in the ties of blood. A society which gives him the possibility of transcending nature by creating rather than destroying it. Building such a society means taking the next step, means the end of humanoid history, the phase in which man had not yet become fully human. It does not mean the end of days. On the contrary, it is man's fate that his existence is beset by contradictions which he has to solve, without ever solving them! He will be confronted with truly human conflicts and problems, have to be adventurous, courageous, imaginative, capable of suffering and of joy, but his powers will be in the service of life, not in the service of death." (Erich Fromm, *The Sane Society*, 1955).

Chapter 3
Spiritual Growth for Social Harmony

To a mind that is still, the whole universe surrenders.

The Buddha

Many would say, perhaps most would say, mankind's affairs are in appalling disarray and humankind has "fallen from grace", behaving sinfully, carelessly, destructively - but all this is totally untrue. The creative programme which is Evolution, regardless of its date of inception, follows a relentless programme of its own, disregarding the whims, fancies and ignorance of us human organisms. Mercifully, some would say! It follows its own laws and has its own methods. One of the dynamic laws of creation is the Law of Cause and Effect, which advocates that what follows at any point in a stage is dependent on what has gone before. Evolution is a continuum of progressive creativeness. Indeed, all the dynamic progress that went before has been the very lead-up on which the energy of the present moment depends for its further propulsion into the future. Under this same law, all that has been gathered from the history of mankind's past to the present day is a reflection of all that went before, and that accumulation is responsible for what happens in our civilisation right <u>now</u>. In this, our MidPoint phase, we are so far along the road, relatively speaking, and with so many resources and so much creative energy that we can and must upscale globally to begin to manifest the very behaviours on which we must depend to sustain our species and our planet.

The Law of Cause and Effect remains stable within an unassailable creative order which will provide Evolution with the structure it needs to fulfil its plan, its only criteria. Failure to recognise that is perilous. We have not the time now to debate it, refute it, ignore it. Better by far to become an Evolution supporter, to wear the rosette. Better still to join the team, the time being perfect in this MidPoint. As humans we do, of course have a choice about what to do and we have procrastinated over what to do, when to do it, how to do it for many years. Now is the time to be bold and take the necessary steps for if we do not, who will?

We do not need knowledge of modern physics to move a switch. We need know little about engineering and electrics to turn an ignition key and get the practical results we expect from our efforts. Living a good life is simple and practical, demonstrable in the perfect setting of which we are all a part. Our human behaviour will take us part of the way and our individual and collective ignorance continues, fortuitously, to be eroded by better and greater paths of knowledge. To continue in our old ways despite the context of present knowledge is to maintain disorder, disbelief, disease, even the destruction of our society, and of ourselves, our souls. We are not only lost, going this way and that, but we are keeping ourselves blindfolded, inhibiting the benefits of the world's creativity and abundance. Our questions should continually be: *Where am I, What can I do now?* rather than: *Should I believe in religion? Can I believe in science? What can I believe in?*

The philosophy of the Mid-Point is based on sanity and serenity, two conditions which present the most perfect environment in which to develop and nurture our species. It is an established philosophy of life to abide by, ensuring diversity and harmony becomes our mantra.

We, the general populace, are mostly confused, even blinded, by intellectual, academic scientific debate. It confuses even scientists themselves at times. Theory is good. Ideas are good. Opinions are good - if they are of practical use. I can only emphasise the importance of practical applied knowledge in the fields of psychology, philosophy, physics, biology, neurology, sociology, criminology, economics, politics, higher education generally so long as it is made to work on behalf of mankind!

If a scientist asks the right questions there is a likelihood he will find an answer but if he tests wider possible outcomes he might not comprehend the answer from amongst the options, even if it was present. Understanding man's connection with reality and his place in the share of life reinforces the significance of the <u>now</u>.

The consequences of choosing to live without recognising our role in the rollout of Evolution are damaging us humans, disturbing our human emotions, our emotional health, endangering our spiritual growth.

The conflict between religious groups throughout our history has been divisive and dysfunctional to our world. Occasionally, some have understood that the Law of Evolution, or Natural Theology, has shaped its imprint on the structure of life in all its forms.

Humans have sometimes shaped both their history and their destiny but by not recognising just what wonderful resources they have for these tasks, they make only poor attempts, and by overlooking the importance of spirituality in the quest for perfection they generate inevitable errors and iterative spirals of behavioural naivety.

Whilst the debate between Creationists and Evolutionists continues apace, it stifles the acceptance and adoption of more advanced thinking, on which humanity's future depends. It has exercised many great minds for centuries and for the reader's ease of understanding I abbreviate many of those in the following pages.

Metaphysical naturalism

Metaphysical naturalism originated in early Greek philosophy (Thales, Anaxagoras, Democritus) because they sought to explain everything by natural causes alone, leading to both the atomic system of Epicureanism which sought to achieve happiness, tranquillity and freedom from fear, and Strato of Lampsacus' philosophy of natural science which expanded the naturalistic elements of Aristotle's thought so that it denied the need for an active god to construct the universe, preferring to place the government of the universe in the unconscious of nature. This latter has led directly to widely advanced forms of physicalism and naturalist pluralism supported by notable contemporary scientific writers such as Mario Bunge, Richard Carrier, Richard Dawkins, Daniel Dennett, Sam Harris and David Mills. Its proposal that nature is all there is and all things supernatural do not exist became, with the rise of Christianity, both heretical and eventually illegal making it difficult to document the history of metaphysical naturalism in the Middle Ages.

Sir Thomas More's seminal book *Utopia* was a critique of the social consequences of greed and was a meditation on the personal cost of entering public service. It describes a community of people living according to the principles of natural law but being receptive to Christian teachings, who reject materialism. It dramatises the difficulties of balancing competing claims of idealism and pragmatism. Drawing on Platonic ideals, the model in turn influenced later philosophical writers such as Huxley, Orwell and Bacon.

Cosmological Argument for Naturalism
_____

"Elegance goes directly to the question of how the laws of nature are constructed. Nobody knows the answer to that. Nobody! It's a perfectly legitimate hypothesis, in my view, to say that some extremely elegant creator made those laws. But I think if you go down that road, you must have the courage to ask the next question, which is: Where did that creator come from? And where did his, her, or its elegance come from? And if you say it was always there, then why

63

not say that the laws of nature were always there and save a step?" Carl Sagan, *Conversations with Carl Sagan,* Tom Head (ed), 2006

Metaphysical naturalists agree that the fundamental constituents of reality, from which everything derives and on which everything depends, are fundamentally mindless. So, if any variety of metaphysical naturalism is true, then any mental properties that exist (and any mental powers or beings) are causally derived from, and ontologically dependent on, systems of non-mental properties, powers or things.

The apparent or conscious physical world takes up almost all our attention. The rest of creative life, the vast, invisible areas of reality are simply ignored, particularly in the Western world, unless we are in a particularly reflective mood. We have accumulated considerable knowledge, some overt and available, some not, certainly more than is generally realised.

Evolution follows a relentless course and cannot entirely be stemmed by us humans although it is being adapted by the metaphysicists, neuroscientists and biochemists to suit their particular life-enhancing ambitions for mankind. It rolls out divergence and choice, working on the basis of perfect equilibrium, inter-coordination and progressive movement. It is controlled by self-adjustment which regulates the on-going creative plan. It makes its own way, so to say, with its own genius so that human intellect will be exemplified in humans whose creative and purposeful direction is determined. Evolution has an overriding purpose. Man has none - yet. Sociologists, psychiatrists, theologians, other experts in social evolution continue to debate if, and how, divine intervention has provided the template for Evolution. It is an endlessly fascinating and awe-inspiring subject.

Nevertheless, Evolution is the most meticulously perfect system that ever existed. It is the blueprint for life because it is life; it is what life is - a process of organised ever-adapting creative development with all energy and intelligence contained in the process itself. We humans are the perpetual defaulters and blame everyone and everything, and even gods of different descriptions for our sad and painful misfortunes. The real truth, the absolute truth, is that there is no blame to be apportioned. It is part of the programme of Evolution that development takes place stage by stage, passing from very near 100% ignorance to 100% knowledge. Eventually we all evolve to the higher states or stages of consciousness or understanding but there is much collaborative and creative work to be done here and now, for everyone, and the great New Age will bring enormous benefits to everyone on the planet.

Taking this to the next aspirational and logical step, we should be seeking common spiritual ground across all our cultures, taking living co-operatively with great humanity to a new universal level of social harmony. A creative Evolutionism.

How, then, do we capture the collective aspirations of humankind to achieve an enlightened destiny, able to free itself to create a more humanitarian civilisation and ensure its own destiny? Uncovering underlying spiritual truths means clearing away all rituals, superstitions mystical notions, which all act like gossip to the enlightenment of the mind. We may see how it is possible to believe that there are dozens of different gods with all sorts of different roles. Or none.

To the many who ask "Does God exist?" the answer is not certain. People who believe in God, believe. People who disbelieve in God, disbelieve. Those who don't know, don't know. Which ones are right? Other ongoing questions continue to tease us: Is God male or female? Of what race? What colour? Is he or she to be loved or feared? It can be argued that in this twenty first century we still cannot be sure that God exists but we can be sure that Evolution exists - the great ongoing power or life force, the energy that is behind all that is: both visible to us humans, as well as invisible. The answer should not be a problem for anyone: from the simple man enjoying the countryside to the greatest scholar or scientist.

"In theory, if a holy book misinterpreted reality its disciples would discover this and the text's authority would be undermined. In practice, however, the power of human cooperation depends on a delicate balance between truth and fiction. Even when scriptures mislead people about the true nature of reality, they retain their authority for

thousands of years. If you distort reality too much it will weaken you so proponents will not be able to compete against more clear-sighted rivals. On the other hand, one cannot organise masses of people effectively without relying on fictional myths: few people would follow. Evidence is persuasive. The Bible peddled a monotheistic theory of history claiming the world is governed by an all-powerful deity who cares above all else about me. If something good happens it must be a reward for good deeds. Any catastrophe must be a punishment for my sins. The Bible doesn't recognise the possibility that droughts/wars/volcanic eruptions arise from a global ecological event, a political system or a powerful economy. Such self-absorption characterises all humans in childhood. Most grow out of such a delusion.

Other religions have a more accurate perception of Earth's history: animist and polytheist religions depict the world with different powers which makes it easier to understand that things happen independently of our own behaviours. In ancient times, Herodotus in Greece or Sima Qian in China understood that wars and revolutions break out due to social, political and economic factors.

Present day scholars would agree with that, and would disagree with the Bible. Modern states invest effort in understanding other cultures: In the USA evangelical Christians will look to China for the cause of their faltering economy, rather than to themselves, yet even today, when US presidents take their oath of office, they place their hand on a Bible" (YN Harari, *Homo Deus*, 2016)

For those who must have a supernatural guide then, to them, I say: make Evolution your god and also reflect that such a god would invent a perfect system for the spawning and development of all that he has created. Whether you are a creationist or an evolutionist, we can all observe the great plan at work at any moment of any day. That is where God is, where Evolution is, and is also where we are.

There is a growing movement called Humanism which promises a non-supernatural basis for meaning and ethics: good without God. Its manifestoes affirm that:

- Knowledge of the world is derived by observation, experimentation and rational analysis;
- Humans are an integral part of nature, the result of unguided evolutionary change;
- Ethical values are derived from human need and interest as tested by experience;
- Life's fulfilment emerges from individual participation in the service of humane ideals;
- Humans are social by nature and find meaning in relationships; and
- Working to benefit society maximises human happiness.

Members of such societies would be the first to insist that the ideals of humanism belong to no sect. Strands of humanism are found in belief systems that go back to the Axial Age, (a term coined by German philosopher Karl Jaspers to refer to the period 500–300 BCE during which most of the main religious and spiritual traditions emerged in Eurasian societies). They came to the fore in the Age of Reason and the Enlightenment, leading to the English, French and American statements of rights, and inspired the United Nations, the Universal Declaration of Human Rights and other institutions of global cooperation.

<u>Now</u> is the great moment: we live in the now, everything is here for us now, we are even part of the great scheme of things now; the world is at our feet. The discoveries of now, the pre-Midpoint, are revolutionary, exciting truths we must gather up in our arms eagerly; great minds and great hearts are there to get matters in better order and show the ways of Evolution. We must engender a great respect for Evolution, a passion for its truth so we can begin the necessary stage of stabilisation to get under way.

Creative Evolutionism was a socialist evolutionist philosophy developed by both George B Shaw and Henri Bergson, deemed to be: *"The genuinely scientific religion for which wise men are now anxiously looking. It makes blood relatives of man, beast and bird; change is driven by a life force pushing matter toward complexity and progress, upward toward the Infinite. It is the 'ghost in the machine' with which humans had better cooperate or they will be swept away with the mammoth and other mistakes".* (Richard Milner, *Encyclopaedia of Evolution,*1900).

Philosopher YN Harari expands this premise in his award winning book *Homo Deus* where he expresses great concern about the West's unawareness of the importance of spirituality:

"Even if we travel all over the globe and study each and every community we would still cover only a fraction of our sapiens mental spectrum. Nowadays, all humans are touched by modernity becoming members of a global village: whether they were influenced by Christian missionaries, European traders, or are wealthy eco-tourists or international researchers.

Shamans, monks, ascetics curiously and systematically explored the mysterious lands of the mind and returned with tales of unfamiliar conscious states, unconscious expansions to infinity and emptiness, and also of supreme tranquillity, sharpness and sensitivity.

The Humanist revolution caused our modern Western culture to lose faith and interest in superior mental states and to sanctify the mundane experiences of the average Joe. Modern Western culture now lacks a specialised class of people seeking to experience extraordinary mental states and anyone attempting to do so is classified as a drug addict, a mental patient or a charlatan. Consequently, we know little about the mental landscapes of North American shamans, Buddhist monks or Sufi mystics.

But that is just the sapiens mind. In probability, there is an infinite variety of mental states that we do not experience. Imagine combining the collective insights of

Neanderthal and other branches of mankind, or harnessing the experiences of other animals?

Thomas Nagel's writings in 1974 about bat echolocation ('What Is It Like to be a Bat?') points out that while the sapiens mind can write algorithms for echolocation systems, it can't tell us how it feels to be a bat, or to feel the echolocation of the moth. Is it the same as seeing it, or is it different? Equally, sapiens cannot understand how it feels to be a different animal: perhaps a pelican or a whale? Both whales and humans process emotions in the limbic part of the brain but the whale's limbic system includes an additional part that is missing from our human structure. Might it equip them to experience deep complex emotions denied to us? Certainly they have both a language of sounds but also an ability to communicate effectively without it, apparently telepathically. Should we be surprised? Sapiens doesn't rule the world because they have deeper emotions or more complex language than other animals but because it has created the machinery to do so: the necessary facilities, drugs, genetic engineering, etc. In the future, brain-computer interfaces being developed may open passages to such places." (YN Harari, *Homo Deus*, 2016).

We can notice the similarity of thought between Harari's futuristic sounding computer–brain interfacing with the socialist Creative Evolutionism of philosophers GB Shaw and Henri Bergson who embraced the concept of man with other species being "as one" in his evolutionary pursuit of perfection.

Issuing a warning note, however, cognitive scientist and psychologist Prof Steven Pinker rejects the idea that ethical traits such as man's tendency towards cooperation and altruism is an indication of divine design, seeing it more as a necessary mechanistic behaviour for survival of large groups, used for both good and evil purposes. He challenges: *"...think Nazis and ISIS: quite the opposite of a collective manifestation of divine intent."*(Steven Pinker, *The Better Angels of Our Nature*, 2011).

Other contemporary writers like geneticist Richard Dawkins are equally convinced:

"Evolution is an inescapable fact. It is within us, around us, between us and its workings are embedded in the rocks of aeons past. What Darwin wouldn't have known, is that comparable evidence becomes more convincing when we include molecular genetics to the anatomical comparisons that were available to him. Just as vertebrae and exoskeletons are invariants of vertebrates and crustaceans so the DNA code is invariant across all living creatures. This astounding fact shows that all living creatures are descended from a single ancestor. When we look at what is written in the code, the actual genetic sequences of all those different creatures, we find the same kind of hierarchical tree of resemblance: the same family tree." (Richard Dawkins, *The Greatest Show on Earth*, 2009).

Even Darwin's ground-breaking evolutionary philosophy included a nod to creationism, conceding that repetitive structures may indeed indicate the presence of God, a unity of purpose offering an intuitive spiritual appeal to the scientific debate.

To summarise, to date, nothing that is not physical has ever been discovered and so metaphysical naturalism remains a valid position based on what is currently known. Empirical methods, especially those of proven use in the sciences, are unsurpassed for discovering the facts of reality, while methods of pure reason alone can securely discover logical errors.

Only by understanding the divergent characteristics of evolutionary development - quite apart from understanding who, or what, is responsible for it - can one put the subject on a rational footing for wide enough investigation. There are obvious advantages of studying the various sciences, but it is the study of mental, emotional, spiritual realms, which also follow exactly the same Laws of Evolution which are actually responsible <u>for</u> Evolution. That has undoubtedly been humans' area of almost sheer neglect which I expand on further in this chapter. Physical and materialistic matters occupy our greater attention, because they are visible and can be manipulated, but the causal forces of Evolution have been neglected. Despite that, we are moving slowly but inexorably into the great next stage in the history of civilisation: the MidPoint.

The restoration of balance displayed in Evolution is like a simple see-saw action. Balance is possible but adjustment is always required. The same dynamic mechanisms used in the whole evolutionary process operate within each living creature – ever able to adjust to the environment, bringing about all the changes to the different species on the planet. There is an all-embracing self-adjusting creativity – not fully known to man, humans can still only observe at this stage of development. Evolution affects all species, and therefore all of us, and we will inexorably all fulfil ourselves and ripen like the cherry on the tree, in its own good time. But we could certainly lend a hand in our own development here!

Those facilities for redressing balance, restoring order and maintaining equilibrium are available to individuals based on their learning journeys from ignorance to knowledge. When an error in our progress is discerned, and we learn from that moment, we have moved forwards as fully and efficiently as we can. Failing to observe the error is a great loss of opportunity both for ourselves and our community as it slows the speed of personal development. This is our built-in self-adjustment device.

My purpose in writing this book is to fly an urgent flag for the need for action, now. This MidPoint is a red alert stage in human Evolution. This is not meant as a criticism. Our failure to address it earlier provides us with the opportunity now to harness new energies to create a better future for later generations – if we will be brave enough now. Up to this MidPoint stage in our Evolution, our civilisation, like those before us, was at its most uncontrollable and traumatic of all stages. We are living an inexplicable life, not knowing why we are here, what we should be doing, or where we are going. Understanding will eventually come to us all but at different times and in different ways. We don't have the luxury of time for that to happen as our global population is soaring and wars, robotics and bioscience developments are throwing up real challenges to humanity.

The process of resolving those traumas defines the MidPoint, the point at which harmonious, spiritual, values are recognised and achieved through the teaching of knowledge and pursuit of transcendental understanding. This MidPoint is the turning point in the history of our civilisation, the time for hard thinking and serious work.

Far more knowledge is available to us than is generally understood. The dichotomy, polarisation, squabbling confusion which permeates our political world makes it difficult to find the truths we will need for a harmonious future. Failure to do this will accelerate the likelihood of human annihilation. Even if this worst possible scenario was to happen, Evolution would continue on, unperturbed, without us, creatively progressing and expanding opportunities for the other species of this planet, and any others in the universe.

We are all familiar with the term New Age and the dawning of the Age of Aquarius. This simply refers to our leaving one Age (the Piscean) and entering a new one (Aquarian). This happens every 2000 years, the last one coinciding with the arrival of Christ. With millennia behind us, an astounding array of skills and competences amongst us, and a pressing need for humanity to harness our potential to achieve a better future for us all, this Age of Aquarius is our MidPoint.

At the moment, the quarter of a million babies reborn every day are born into a world where there is uncertainty and indecision, and no universal basic structure for living, no uncontested standards or values, and no unanimously agreed principles to live by. It is a universal problem. Although each baby reborn is thought by many to be more advanced as each has a greater knowledge relatively to previous rebirths, the rules and regulations of the prevailing society into which he or she is born have a powerful effect on the mental reactions of the new life as it seeks to recapitulate and regain its bearings.

The first principle to be mastered by each of us here on this planet is that of complete Unity, which is the Law of Love Unto All Beings, stemming from our awareness that the Earth is alive and all of life is sacred and interconnected. Each of us embodies the divine. Our ultimate spiritual authority is within and we need no other person to interpret the sacred to us when remembering that Evolution's mystery goes beyond physical form.

All this has been inevitable during the pre-MidPoint as there has been insufficient knowledge: the compounding of human error upon human error, and the blinding conflict and frustration of the opposites has kept society entangled in chaos. When we understand the wholeness of everything there is and our continuity in the whole Evolutionary process, we lose our fears and insecurity which bring about such deteriorations of the whole person. Evolution is in charge, whether we like it or not, or whether we realise it or not.

That is the foundation of the MidPoint stage: the collation of knowledge and equivalent reduction in ignorance, and the drawing up of mankind's blueprint for his future. His destiny demands it! His life physically depends on it, because without the workshop of physical existence the soul of man cannot survive. The spiritual is contained in the physical - it can only manifest itself and flourish in the cut-and-thrust of life, in the conflicting experiences from which grains of truth can be assimilated, the essences of life as they become understood in our pursuit of understanding knowledge about our soul.

If the ways of the post-MidPoint were incomprehensible to mankind in his pre-MidPoint stage, the pathway through the New Age now will be equally hard to assimilate. Usually knowledge is developed gradually stage by stage, an evolutionary movement from ignorance to knowledge, but at this MidPoint it is essential for our "sufficient" knowledge from across all the disciplines and across all cultures to be brought together most rapidly, and shared for our universal good.

Although there are many divisions of opinion on almost all subjects of our human world this is only because of the diversity of knowledge and also experience that each of us has. We mistakenly divide everything up into seeming opposites of thought; the talk of good and bad, right and wrong, we should do this and we should not do that. It is a knowledge revolution – perhaps shocking, perhaps exciting and inspiring, and certainly challenging. The whole balance of life as we know it is teetering, exciting fear, anxiety, power-grabs: a positive earthquake of all feelings as we shift from known ignorance to unexplored unions of spiritual and secular advancement. Overwhelming perhaps, especially when the sum of so much knowledge could arrive collectively at the same historic moment, when humankind may find itself wanting and newly aware of its collective ignorance.

Constructivity starts to replace destructivity in the New Age, the MidPoint revolution point. The new perspective must be glimpsed, like a fresh inspiration, and must form the basis for continuance of the species, which has come about purposefully, with power, direction and manifests all the powers of The Intelligence, inner and outer. We all have our inner world, our inner mental life. It is what we are exploring at this moment. But there is an outer world too and we have to move away from ignorance in both realms. We must know ourselves better to understand the world better, and to help ourselves collectively aspire to achieve our societies' potential. It is all the same reality of which mankind is part, always has been and always will be. Without perspective and self-identification we remain in the darkness of ignorance.

You have no grounds for negating yourself at any time. Nor do you have grounds for imagining you are in some way more elevated than you actually are. You are as you are. That is fine. It is your behaviour that probably needs consideration! That too is based on your ignorance/knowledge level as it stands today. That is the crux of the matter. We mustn't grandiose ourselves with pretences, or condemn ourselves too easily or we will become unnecessarily depressed or depleted, when the reality of the situation does not call for such.

Discovery of, release of, and development of the unrestricted potential of the soul of the individual, is a flow-through from transcendental understanding, understood as such, all to do with the unseen, invisible, vibrations or creative forces of Evolution, electro-dynamic forces from source of origin. This will all become part of the New Age curriculum for children and adults alike: the Enlightenment of the MidPoint era, a gigantic revolution.

It is important to recognise just how much the ideas of sin and godliness have been embedded in our consciousness and how suffused we are by the concepts of God and the Devil, good and evil. It all implies that man has failed as a socialised group because there is no perfection or godliness in our behaviour. As individuals, our souls must have fallen and as a result we are sinners. Religion has supported this view, deliberately creating the fear of Hell and fiery death in agonising circumstances to blackmail non-believers into choosing God's ways. There is much of this in religious indoctrination. The civilisation of mankind has based its philosophy on this powerful opposite – and it still limits us.

Although Creationists like to believe that 6000 years ago all living things came into existence in a single week, Evolution is an inescapable reality:

"It is within us, around us, between us and its workings are embedded in the rocks of aeons passed. Given that we don't live long enough to watch evolution happen we shall use the metaphor at the scene of a crime after the event, and making inferences. The detective has no hope of witnessing the actual crime, what he has is traces that remain. There are footprints, bloodstains, letters, diaries. The aids to inference which lead scientists to the fact of evolution are far more numerous, more convincing, more incontrovertible than any eye witness reports that have

ever been used in any court of law, in any century, to establish guilt in any crime. Proof beyond reasonable doubt! Reasonable doubt? That is the understatement of all time! At the same time, paradoxically, ill-informed opposition is even stronger than I can ever remember. What would be evidence against evolution, and very strong evidence at that, would be the discovery of even a single fossil in the wrong geological stratum. Sceptics wishing to prove their case should be diligently scrabbling around in rocks trying to find anachronistic fossils. They haven't." (Richard Dawkins, *The Greatest Show on Earth,* 2009

The great law of Evolution is this: It is impossible for man to make a mistake. Evolution does not sustain mistakes. Consequently no man has made, or can make, a mistake. With the opposites ignorance and knowledge – and clearly both exist - no person can behave any 'better' than his ignorance allows him to and therefore, collectively, no society can lose its knowledge.

So, in our exciting New Age, does free will actually exist or is everything pre-ordained in a template? For centuries, theologians have debated the relationship between the soul and the will. The soul being the true self, the essence of man, of you and me. Deciding this is more than just a philosophical exercise. If organisms lack free will it implies we can manipulate and control all desires using psychological therapies, drugs, genetic engineering, brain surgery: neurones being fired because they are stimulated artificially, rather than through our own biology. Whilst it is discomforting to our vanity to accept such a premise, equally, relegating the behaviours of humans to a mere neural pulsation is too intellectually lazy to accept as the blueprint for our future development.

Can we be sure that our perception of ourselves as a single self, who can distinguish our unique desires from others' influences, is not just a welcome liberal myth which is, now, openly challenged by neuroscientists and behavioural psychologists?

Professor Alexander Rosenberg, fellow at the National Humanities Centre, expresses the position that naturalists in general have to accept moral nihilism:

"Many naturalists are compatible with regard to human free will, believing that humankind can choose to do what it wants, and in many cases, even choose their desire. However, choices are ultimately constrained by the physical and biological realities of circumstances, and our nature as human beings, for example, we cannot choose to violate the laws of physics or be smarter than we are, and some of our desires relate to unalterable features of nature as human beings. Nevertheless, once we accept the limitations of our physical world and bodies, our will is not constrained by much else than knowledge, desire and powers of reasoning so we can indeed choose what we do."(Alexander Rosenberg, *The Atheist's Guide to Reality: Enjoy Life without Illusions*, 2011.)

Mind as Pure Intelligence

Liberation is not anything new for it is already waiting, already an option, only to be realised. Such realisation arises with the elimination of ignorance. Absolutely nothing more is required to achieve the aim of life. Mind divested of thought becomes pure intelligence and is identified with the self and destroys ignorance. Being within the universe cannot be different from consciousness. The two things would not be able to co-exist within the same limits.

Objective knowledge is gained by the mind and the mind is not, and cannot yet be, objectified. It follows therefore that the mind exists even in the absence of objects. Such pure mind is entirely divested of all knowledge or thoughts and is pure intelligence.

Pure intelligence free from objective knowledge has been proved to exist. It can be felt on reflective occasions in ordinary life as well as in meditative states. It goes largely undetected because people are not conversant with it, but transcendence will reveal it.

If the body is transcended and the self is realised even once, there ensues that wisdom which will eradicate ignorance and override the cycle of births and deaths. Liberation is not to be sought in heaven or earth or in the nether regions, it is synonymous with self-realisation.

If one's mind, or rather one's identity and existence as a person, is entirely the product of natural processes, according to determinist philosopher W.T. Stace (1886-1967), three assumptions must follow: First, if there is no free will, there is no morality. All mental contents (such as ideas, theories, emotions, moral and personal values, or aesthetic responses) exist solely as computational constructions of one's brain and genetics, not as things that exist independently of these. Second, damage to the brain (regardless of how it derived) should be of great concern. Third, death or destruction of one's brain cannot be survived, which is to say, all humans are mortal. Given the inevitability of physical death which entails our complete extinction with no evidence of afterlife, humans must accept their mortality.

Further, Stace believes that ecstatic mysticism calls into question the assumption that awareness is impossible without mental processing. (WT Stace, *Mysticism and Philosophy*, 1960)

The seismograph has already detected the initial tremors of what is to be. In this MidPoint we face huge humanistic crises: terrorism, ecological disasters, greater uncertainty about humanity's future. Isn't now the very time to harness humanity's hope and collective altruism?

Enlightenment can only exist within purity: purity of order, of harmony, of truth and of beauty. It is a meticulously creative programme of which we are all a part. The basic laws of connection which direct and manifest our individual creations in terms of gifts, talents, potentialities are just not understood although there is sufficient knowledge available in the numerous disciplines to form an integrated picture, and the blueprint for human living can now be formulated and established for the whole of society as a basic structure.

The leaders of New Age thought in all their forms have provided, for many years, the teachings needed to help ourselves release our creative potential to its fullest within the evolutionary system of which we are an essential part. Love of life and self and others in its fullest and finest forms are the rightful emotions for the New Age civilisation, possible, now, for the first time as we move beyond the stage of confusion, hate and violence we experienced pre-MidPoint.

Humans evolved as social animals, which is why we developed the diverse cultures and civilisations on which we now depend. Humans, having been "programmed" by nature, require a healthy society in order to flourish and to feel happy and content, which means the pursuit of human happiness requires the pursuit of a healthy society to live in, to interact with, and to benefit from.

The glimpse of the error gives us the appropriate enlightenment. Consider that each individual's birth from a single sperm to becoming a biologically complex adult actually mimics Evolution itself, from its emergence from the swamp to the homo sapiens we recognise. In fact, in every animal's development from embryo to its adult form, it changes more significantly than in purely evolutionary terms, through the generations.

Man tries to shape both his history and his destiny, but by not knowing just what wonderful resources he has for this objective, he makes a poor attempt, and sometimes the inevitable errors bring additional problems and complications, which only induce further errors.

Humans' choices are ultimately constrained by their physical and biological forms and their nature as human beings, as uniquely developed individuals. Some of our desires are manifestations of unalterable features of our DNA, others are ingrained features of our character and only alterable with considerable conscious effort. Nevertheless whilst we accept the limitations of our physical world, our will is not constrained by much else than our knowledge, wants, desires, powers of reasoning within the limitations of what we know, or can think of. We can indeed choose what to do, on the basis of a rational or intuitive analysis of the possible.

If we start with a negative concept, every thought and emotion derived will be negative. Further forward thinking will attract even more negative thinking and those negative thoughts, feelings and actions will ultimately bring us to the end of a woeful cul-de-sac, and what a rough personal journey it will be!

Chapter 4
A New Human Agenda

My passionate concern for our common destiny draws the thinking part of life ever further onward. In principle there is no feeling which has a firmer foundation in nature, or greater power. But in fact there is also no feeling which awakens so belatedly, since it can become explicit only when our consciousness has expanded beyond the broadening, but still far too restricted, circles of family, country and race, and has finally discovered that the only truly natural and real human Unity is the Spirit of Earth.

Pierre Teilhard de Chardin, *Building the Earth*, 1965

We are on the fringe of intellectual and spiritual freedom, bound by fewer religious and social restraints than any time in the past. True spirituality is our interactivity with the invisible, but very real, matter of existence.

The Laws of Evolution, when we can locate them, can reveal the absolute truths which we now recognise, understand and respect because they reveal scientifically the dynamic processes of the whole creative system. We accept that we are part of the great system controlled by these natural laws, nothing more than the dynamic forces working through our physical body. We also understand these laws are fully established and dynamically operative within and about us as, equally, we accept we are part of a larger whole. Thus, there are ethical challenges: collectiveness not separation, unity not disunity, creative order not disorder, ongoing progress not restriction and inhibition, and integration not disintegration.

Epigenesis is the name given to the concept that since humankind is born with a mind, it is this original creative impulse which has been the cause of all mankind's development by building upon that which has already been created but adding new elements to become creative intelligences. Spiritual evolution, or higher evolution, is the philosophical, esoteric ideal that nature and human beings can evolve, either as a concept of established cosmological patterns or in accordance with pre-established potentials, differentiating psychological, mental and spiritual evolution from the lower, biological evolution of physical form. Within this broad definition, theories of spiritual evolution are very diverse but one can regard all of them as teleological to some degree:

- Cosmological: describing existence at large;
- Personal: describing development of the individual;
- Holistic: holding that higher realities emerge from, and are not reducible to, the lower;
- Idealist: holding that the reality is primarily mental or spiritual;
- Non-dual: holding that there is no ultimate distinction between mental and physical reality.

Many renowned philosophers, scientists and educators have proposed theories of spiritual evolution - Schelling, Hegel, Jung, Theon, Rudolph Steiner, Teilhard de Chardin, Barfield, Schumacher, Sarkar, Skumin, Wilber and Swimme, among others.

This MidPoint is the turning point in the history of our civilisation, the time for hard thinking and serious collaborations towards defining and sustaining that future. Obviously we have no knowledge of the future. None of us can have as it does not yet exist. We create it when we release ourselves to it but, here is the paradox, we are actually in it all the time!

Can it be that simple, to devise meta-solutions to meet all our society's needs? The human brain has three principal structures. The largest is the cerebrum and is the centre for intellectual functioning, or reasoning. The second is the cerebellum, located at the back of the skull which helps us stand upright. The third structure is the medulla, a stem leading to the spinal column which helps to handle involuntary tasks like respiration. These three structures work together to help carry out the role of cognition, but they are not the mind itself. Mind is not a physical entity.

British Social Attitudes surveys, run annually since 1983, include a question about which religion or denomination people consider they belong to. In 1983 32% said they belonged to no religion. In 2015 it rose to 49% and in 2016 it was 53%, with much of that increase being attributed to young people.

In contrast, Humanist Societies are increasing their memberships, their stated aim being:*"to see a world where everyone lives co-operatively in a secular world based on shared human values, respect for human rights and concern for future generations"*. It seems a little bland. I would advocate a more proactive strategy - for developing and protecting all future generations.

"History does not tolerate a vacuum. As famine, plague and war are decreasing in the twenty first century, something else will take their place. We had better think carefully otherwise we may gain victory in old battlefields

only to be caught unawares on new fronts. What shall we strive for – immortality, happiness, divinity? A central project will be to protect humankind from the dangers inherent in our own power. We do not usually need to pray to any god or saint to rescue us, we know quite well what needs to be done and we usually succeed in doing it." (YN Harari, *Homo Deus*, 2016).

Educationalist Rudolph Steiner supported the view that before the MidPoint of our Earth's Evolution human beings did not possess freedom of choice between good and evil, proposing that whilst we could talk about good and evil in the subordinate kingdoms of nature, it would be ridiculous to discuss whether a mineral wanted to crystallise, a lily to blossom, a lion to kill. So, only with man, in our phase of Evolution, can we speak about what we call freedom of choice. Only to human beings do we ascribe the capacity to distinguish between good and evil.

Why do individuals, gangs, even nations, develop hostile, anti-social outlooks when we are all distant cousins, all part of the family, all eager to live the good life in the happiest and most beneficial manner? The basic problem is that too many of us are all flying blind with no knowledge of the grand purpose of the fantastic life we are living. We make up our reasons for living and we have different ideas on the matter. People are working to "prove themselves", to "be a success", to "reach the top", to "be famous", to "be very powerful". All these are thought to be commendable signs of personal achievement and evidence that a society is dynamic, economically thriving - but it fails to harness the spiritual, emotional, social yearnings of its peoples.

Our imagination must now focus sharply and clearly on shaping a collaborative civilisation: a humane, creative, aspirational, spiritual society. If mankind hopes to achieve any level of perfection, it will be necessary to have a clear image of the perfection it is trying to reach.

Evolution: The Maturation of Homo Sapiens

Jung referred to *"a disease of the soul longing to become whole"* when explaining anxieties and neuroses.

We think about life from the social position we fit into, and we use the ideas of that class and environment and absorb the opinions and beliefs of the day. These provide us with our own customised set of blinkers!

Being free from self-destructive behaviour is not merely an abstract concept; rather it is a real possibility. Being fully functional is within our grasp, and complete mental present-moment health can be a choice. This section is devoted to the description of the ideal, mature human personality whose healthy minds and behaviours are not self-centred and self-limiting but selfless and displaying an enviable ability to be creatively alive at every moment.

Such healthy people behave differently from the tribal and consensual unthinkingness of the masses:

they possess distinct qualities, outside the conventions of racial, socio-economic or sexual stereotypes. They do not fit neatly into any roles, job descriptions, geographic patterns, educational levels or financial statistics. There is a different quality about them, but the difference is not discernible in the traditional external factors by which we usually classify people. How is it possible to recognise such a person?

These healthy people live now, rather than in the past or the future. They are not threatened by the unknown, and they seek out experiences that are new and unfamiliar to them. They savour "the now" at all times, aware that this is all they have. The moments between events are just as liveable as those taken up by the events themselves, and they have an uncanny ability to get every pleasure out of their daily lives. They gather in their happiness now, and then when the future now arrives, they gather in that one as well. These individuals are always enjoying now because they see the folly of waiting to enjoy.

Most obviously, you see people who like virtually everything about life, people who are comfortable doing just about anything and waste no time in complaining, or wishing that things were otherwise. They are enthusiastic about life, and they want all they can get out of it. They like picnics, movies, books, sport, concerts, cities, farms, animals, mountains and just about everything. They like life. When you are around someone like this you will notice the absence of grumbling, moaning, or even passive sighing. If it rains they like it. If it's hot they love it, never complaining about it. If they are in a traffic jam, or at a party, or all alone, they simply deal with what is there. There is no pretending to enjoy, but a sensible acceptance of what is, and an outstanding ability to delight in that reality. Ask them what they don't like and they are hard pressed to come up with an honest answer. While such annoyances as diseases, droughts, mosquitoes, floods and the like are not warmly embraced by such people, they never spend any of their present moments complaining about them, or wishing they weren't so. If situations need to be eradicated, they will work at eradicating them – and enjoy the work.

Healthy fulfilled people are free from guilt and all the attendant anxieties that go with using any present moments in paralysis over past events. Certainly they can admit to making mistakes, and they may vow not to repeat certain behaviour that is counter-productive in any way, but they do not waste their time wishing they hadn't done something, or being upset because they dislike something that they did at an earlier moment in their lives. Complete freedom from guilt is one hallmark of a healthy individual. No lamenting the past and no attempt to make others choose guilt by asking such inane questions as "Why didn't you do it differently?" or "aren't you ashamed of yourself?" They see that feeling bad in the present moment reinforces a poor self-image, and that learning from the past is far superior to remonstrating about the past.

These healthy people are strikingly independent, and while they may have a strong love and devotion for the family, they see independence as superior to dependence in all relationships. They treasure their own freedom from expectations. Their relationships are based on mutual respect for the right of an individual to make decisions for him or herself. Their love involves no imposition of values on the loved one. They put a high premium on privacy, which may make others feel snubbed or rejected. They like to be alone at times and they will go to great lengths to see that their privacy is protected. While they enjoy others and want to be with them, they want even more for others to make it without crutches or leaning. They refuse to be dependent, or depended upon, in a mature relationship. With children they provide a model of a caring person, but they encourage self-reliance almost from the very beginning with a great amount of love offered at every turn.

You will find an uncommon absence of approval-seeking in these happy, fulfilled individuals. They are able to function without approval or applause from others. They do not seek out honours as most people do. They are unusually free from the opinion of others, almost uncaring whether someone else likes what they have said or done. They do not attempt to shock others, or to gain their approval. These are people who are so internally directed that they are literally unconcerned about others' evaluation of their behaviour.

These are people who accept themselves without complaint. They know that they are human beings, and that being so involves certain human attributes. They know that they look a certain way, and they accept it. They've accepted themselves, and therefore they are the most natural of people. No hiding behind artificialities, no apologising for what they are. They don't know how to be offended by anything that is human. Similarly, they accept all of nature for what it is, rather than wishing it were otherwise. They never complain about things that won't change, such as heat waves, rainstorms or cold water. They accept themselves and the world as it is.

They have insight into the behaviour of others, and what may seem complex and indecipherable to others, they see as clear and understandable. The problems that immobilise so many others are often viewed as only minor annoyances by these people. This lack of emotional involvement in problems makes them able to surmount obstacles that remain insurmountable to others. They have insight into themselves, too, and they recognise immediately what others are attempting to do for them. They can shrug and ignore while others are angered and immobilised. They are never perplexed or stumped and what may seem to be confusing and insoluble to most others is often viewed by them as a simple condition with a ready resolution. They are not focussed on problems in their emotional world. For these people a problem is really only an obstacle to be overcome rather than a reflection on what they are or aren't as a person. Their self-worth is located within, and therefore any external concerns can be viewed objectively, rather than as in any way a threat to their value. This is a most difficult trait to understand since most people feel easily threatened, and this very characteristic may make them threatening to others.

So, how do we go about replicating the best characteristics of homo sapiens to create a future in which we can all thrive and bring the collective benefits of shared understanding to all our communities and their future generations?

The Need for a New Form of Education

Humans stand supreme, the highest expression of living nature only because of our mind. It is our mind which lifts us above the animal kingdom. The question is, do we rightly deserve this honour? We have abused our potential by failing to use it well. We have learned and taught the wrong things and behaved in destructive ways. This is not because we do not know it is wrong, rather it is because we behave to suit our own ends and without civic responsibility. Whilst our minds have, biologically, grown through the ages, our knowledge of how to use them has remained at a despairingly elementary level.

There is little meaning or purpose in the average person's life because meaning and purpose have not been explained, or explored. Little wonder if morality is at a low ebb and non-ethical conduct appals us. For most people life's goal is not discernible. Instead there is a restless groping, an idle drifting, a surging to nowhere. Such a state brings insecurity and because of this, an unhealthy desire for personal gain. The beautiful, truthful, dynamic, creative qualities within us all are shut away in the dark recesses of our ignorance.

One significant factor of modern schooling models stands out which is the absence of any systematic form of mind training or character training. Neither are such areas of development expected of parents as part of their child rearing process. Indeed many parents will expect that schools should undertake this responsibility whilst schools will put the onus on parents and the home environment. Neither can take responsibility however because society is constantly evolving in a piecemeal way, without any model for civic behaviour.

A system of mind development should in fact begin in our early lives and become established on practical, socially effective lines, and educationalists must take the initiative. Principles of practical and applied psychology can be taught to children, using suitable terminology befitting their age and understanding and should become part of a new standard of education.

The subjects taught should enable children to become good at planning, clear thinking, able to compare and contrast data, prepare an argument, debate issues and converse articulately and easily, write fluently and generally to be confident in different social settings.

Once such children realise they can systematically develop the gifts, talents and abilities innate within themselves to become creative, positive, successful adults there is no doubt they would be highly motivated to do so. Once he or she realises they have such forces within themselves, this would of itself create a sense of purpose and potential achievement. They would have learned the benefits of developing a positive, creative attitude towards their own lives and would go on to develop a philosophical approach to their environment, to others, to the life evolving around them.

In recent years, I confess that when I see a new-born baby I am inclined to think of it as a "creative instrument" just waiting to be nurtured and shaped to the best of its potential, to release its gifts and talent which can be exploited for the benefit of us all. In reply to the critics who express the view this is a cold-blooded attitude I say "No", to fail to do so is to undermine the very special and unique opportunities afforded us by our Evolution.

Children and adults need a motivation to learn but I believe the desire for self-development and personal improvement and success is inherent in every one of us, needing only a trigger. Growth according to the Laws of Evolution will then take place.

The Value of Classical Humanist Education (*source: Petrach Institute*)

The *studia humanitatis* formed the backbone of the Western educational tradition from at least the Renaissance. During the twentieth century, however, this ideal came under increasing strain as a result of revolutionary changes in educational practice. One striking measure of this was the declining role of the classics in higher education. As an example, in 1838 Harvard University's entrance exam requirement was for fluent knowledge of Cicero and Virgil, and the required undergraduate curriculum covered advanced Greek and Latin composition and the study of figures like Xenophon, Sophocles, Homer, Horace and Livy.

In the course of the twentieth century however, the classics lost their status as the foundation of universal education and were demoted to a rather recondite and increasingly rare field left to specialists. Certainly there were positive aspects to the broader understanding of the humanities that moved beyond a narrow focus on the ancient Roman and Greek cultures. Yet even the humanities in our broader contemporary sense felt an accelerating sense of decline. Statistics cited in an April 2010 article in *The Chronicle of Higher Education* showed the percentage of humanities majors in the US had dropped to just 8% of the study body from 17.8% in the 1960s. While politicians frequently lament illiteracy in the sciences and mathematics, they seldom take note of the absence of basic literacy in fields such as history.

According to a study entitled *Still at Risk* conducted in 2008 by the Adult Education Institute, a majority of 17 year old high school students in the US could not place the US Civil War in the correct time period, nearly 40% could not identify the Renaissance and nearly a quarter could not identify Adolf Hitler.

The crisis of the humanities appears to stem partly from an ever growing utilitarian concept of education. According to this view, the goal of university and higher education is to provide those marketable technical skills necessary for practical success in the world – most especially in a chosen career. From this perspective, advanced studies in science, engineering, technology or economics seems far more relevant than the five traditional disciplines of the *studia humanitatis:* philosophy, history, rhetoric, poetry and Greek and Latin grammar. Judged in terms of use-value it might seem reasonable to argue that courses in business accounting and computer programming represent more pressing concerns than mastering Plato and Virgil. All of these claims raise a formidable challenge to defenders of the humanist ideal of education, posing the question "What exactly is the value of humanist education?"

It is interesting that the liberal ideal of education arose originally from an intensely practical concern among the Sophists, who first developed this system of education as an art of good citizenship. In despotic societies an educated citizenry was of little import; absolute kings and tyrants after all ruled by force or decree. In societies like Greece and Rome, however, citizens were expected to take part in actively ruling. As Pericles noted in his famous Funeral Oration, the Athenians were unique amongst nations in regarding the man who was uninvolved in public affairs not as harmless but as useless. Rhetoric was therefore, for the Sophists, the principal foundation of a liberal education. To be a good and active citizen required a broad and expansive knowledge of many issues, an ability to use and understand logic and argument, and the ability to employ language persuasively. In contemporary Western societies which have inherited this Graeco-Roman ideal of the free, and responsible, citizen, this is no less true. In this sense, therefore, liberal education does have an important pragmatic component.

The philosophers of ancient Greece, however, deepened and challenged the Sophistic idea of education and tended toward a more idealistic understanding that struck at utilitarianism itself:

"We ought not to sail to the Pillars of Hercules and run many dangers for the sake of wealth, while we spend neither labour nor money for wisdom. Verily it is slavish to long for life, instead of for the good life... and to seek the

money but pay no attention whatever to the noble." (Aristotle, *Protrepticus.*)

In short, the purely utilitarian view of education confuses ends with means. It presumes that wisdom and knowledge must serve some purpose beyond themselves, such as to enable the acquisition of wealth or position, whereas in fact for Aristotle wisdom and knowledge are ends in themselves. As he says in the opening of Metaphysics *"All men by nature desire to know"*. If one asks then why thus the pursuit of wisdom is worthy, Aristotle would reply that it fulfils and develops what is noble and proper to man: his reason.

Perhaps the strongest pragmatic argument for the humanist education ideal is that it is a *universal* form of education which aims at the fullest development of human faculties. Technical education equips a person with specific skills to perform particular tasks but the fully developed person is often the one best equipped to perform any task. The habits of mind which develop the capacity for critical and creative thought are useful in virtually any situation. *"Those who, having come far and having long found a nursing mother in philosophy, turn afterwards to other interests in life, whether the civil law be their pursuit, or the service of the state in peace and war maybe sure that, to whatever they devote themselves, they will take with them an increased store both of facility in entering and of wisdom and determination in fulfilling their task. Those who make their abiding habitation in philosophy are to be deemed godlike rather than of the common way and nature of man."* (Cardinal Sadoleto, *De Pueris Recte Instituendis.)*

In 2002, English educationalists developed a teaching module for secondary schools exploring civic responsibilities following a concerted campaign from politicians of all parties concerned that citizenship education should be part of the mainstream secondary curriculum, offering a broad and balanced focus on matters of national and international debate. It is also studied as a non-core subject within England's primary schools.

At about the same time, an innovative learning model was developed by philosopher Matthew Lipman: Philosophy for Children, a late twentieth century model of learning a student-led enquiry based approach to learning. This is a pedagogic approach that centres on teaching thinking skills and the ability of students to question and reason. It was drawn from the rich genre of Western philosophy, particularly Socrates, and Dewey school of psychology, notably the Vygotskian theory of social construction. Professor Lipman was concerned with the Deweyan notion of creating an education for a healthy democracy – an education that would develop a critical citizenry with respect and empathy for others in the community. The model is called "Community of Enquiry" and the community network aspect is considered of equal importance to the philosophical enquiry as it uses stories to stimulate challenging questions from young people which helps them to reason and reflect. He proposes this makes it particularly suitable for twenty first century learning which he believes runs the risk of becoming even more individualistic and instrumental.

Philosophy for Children (P4C) is resourced by Sapere, (Sapere.org.uk) a training organisation teaching teachers and other educators in the uses of this model, but it has not, and neither have others like it, been adopted as a mainstream teaching technique within our school system.

Humanistic Approach to Child Development and Psychology

The Humanistic Approach is a system in which human values and interests are of primary importance. This personality-centred approach is an element of the humanistic movement which arrived during the1960s and 1970s. Humanistic psychologists including Abraham Maslow and Carl Rogers criticised Freud and other psychologists because of their focus on emotional disturbance rather than the holistic personality.

Carl Rogers initially studied agriculture but abandoned it to pursue divinity and during his explorations of the world his religious views changed from fundamental to liberal, encapsulated in his personality theory *Development of the Self in Childhood,* that *"The core of human nature is positive"*. He proposed there are three parts to the development of the self: Positive Regard, Conditions of Worth and Incongruence.

During the Positive Regard stage of development children seek for love, approval and acceptance from others, especially their mothers. Rogers recognised that when the positive regard is unconditional the mother's love is freely granted, not conditional on the child's behaviour. However, when it is conditional we must seek other ways of forming positive regard for ourselves. The stage Conditions of Worth reflects a similarity to Freud's superego. During this stage, we see ourselves as worthy only if the conditions are acceptable to our parents and we avoid behaviours or conditions that are unacceptable to them. The final stage, Incongruence, describes the development of self between self-concept and behaviours which threaten our self-image. His work was seminal in influencing psychology with client-centred techniques although he has been criticised for failing to recognise the impact of unconscious forces, or self-actualisation, within his personality theory.

The Child as a Person

"This point may seem trivial and obvious but a look into the history of childhood, institutions, neglect and abuse will show that children have often been treated as non-persons, or objects. The idea of the 'person' implies the recognition of each child's uniqueness with an individual's specific

experiential enjoyment, history and genetic constitution. At the same time, it implies pan-human similarity because despite cultural differences the human child shares the same fundamental needs, and for that reason humans have a common basis for reciprocal understanding.

From this point of view, a child's need is not only for sustenance and survival, love and security, it also includes the need for dignity and self-respect. As a child grows older he or she develops a self-identity and agency based on the codes of respect in the local community. Treating a child as a person involves recognition and confirmation of the need for respect and dignity as opposed to humiliation and disrespect. Implicit in a humanistic approach is also the idea of compassionate participation and understanding of our shared human existence and destiny, where we all are at some stage vulnerable and helpless. For that reason, humans have the potential to understand and react humanely to others in a similar situation." (Bauman 1966, Hoffman 2000, Vetlesen 1999)

Early New Age training in Evolution will help keep the soul in its basic equilibrium so when there is a traumatic imbalance or disturbance the child will more easily regain equilibrium, minimising the chances of drastic traumatic disturbance and consequential longer term social, mental or physical imbalance.

At the top of the hierarchy, for we are not all equally competent, are the men and women of greatness, the geniuses, the inspired original thinkers who are now leading us into the future.

Einstein, when he looked back on his early phase of living, considered with regret that he had not expressed himself with sufficient clarity. He did not explain precisely what he had come to understand, when he said: "*Imagination is more important than knowledge. It is the prime factor in our lives.*" We cannot do anything without at first having the knowledge to bring it about, but the power of the imagination is imperative in all we humans do, if we are to achieve greater things. Inasmuch as it was imagination that took man to the moon, without knowledge and information it would not have been possible. Today, in this New Age, we have sufficient knowledge for our next stage of history. Ignorance is a black void – knowledge illuminates and fires the imagination for greater enlightenment. Evolution works on the basis of perfect equilibrium, inter-coordination, and progressive movement. It is all controlled from "base". The force of universal creation which we call Intelligence is its essence.

There is no limit to the knowledge we may absorb. Blockages to learning may be overturned through psychological therapies, embracing the role of the family in educating our children for the futures they will face.

We are losing the ability to dream, to remember dreams, to move lucidly within them and control our actions, even to travel to higher planes of existence or meet visitors from other worlds as the modern world dismisses dreams as subconscious messages at best and mental garbage at worst. Whatever is the question, the answer is found within ourselves.

It is so easy to condemn the world as being self-indulgent and too materialistic, too irresponsible – but it takes time to become responsible – and responsible to what we must ask. The answer is Evolution.

The first priority must be the family.

"Man is not rightly conditioned until he is a happy, healthy and prosperous being, and happiness, health and prosperity are the result of harmonious adjustment to the inner with the outer, of the man with his surroundings. The world is your kaleidoscope, the varying combinations of colours at every succeeding moment present to you the exquisitely adjusted picture of your ever-moving thoughts." (James Allen, *As a Man Thinketh*, 1903).

The child sees the differences between male and female and respects both. When a child feels satisfied and is comfortable within itself, it does not develop envy, jealousy, greed. There is nothing to resent or be suspicious of, just family unity, which is all that is needed, and there will be cooperation with others outside the immediate family with reciprocal integration being experienced by all concerned.

There are obvious standards for "good enough" parenting: they need to love each other, be sufficiently confident of themselves and of each other to offer a safe place and a future where their babies can grow and learn. You would not take a car on a motorway without learning to drive and if you did there would be repercussions, and there would be punishment. Sometimes drivers have to be protected from themselves in order to protect the rest of us!

Equally, every human has the capacity to be an excellent person but each of us needs to learn social skills and personal assurance. We each owe it to ourselves to find a mate with whom to share life's opportunities, including our own sexual development, for lovemaking is the greatest art of all from which all other arts derive. Ultimately, and at their own maturity, most will yearn to have family of their own to pass on their heritage.

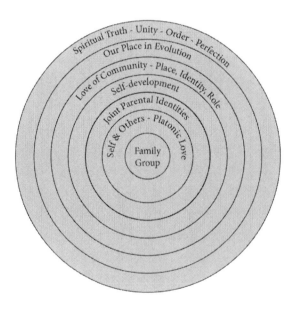

Children must not be sent out into a confused world to work out for themselves the rules and responsibilities of belonging to it. Well laid-down plans of life and human loving and living must be taught to children as soon as they can understand, in ways they can understand to guide their development and best possible personal growth:

- By explaining the story of Evolution, the beauty of nature, the truths of science.

- By taking part in sports and games to promote healthy physical development.

- By clearly explaining about procreation and birth.

- Teaching psychology to explain human behaviour and our development potential.

- Encouraging their own potential, their strengths and opportunities: their personal responsibility for healthy self-management, their attitudes to others and their own achievements; compassion and responsibility for others.

- By learning the languages, technologies, histories, literature, arts and sciences of diverse cultures to gain a wide understanding of the world.

- By exercising spiritual awareness to suit both age and experience, to fulfil the widest potential: training should always encourage originality at all levels in a variety of ways, to distinguish creation from imitation.

- Appreciating differences: strengths, experiences, cultures and knowledge.
- Learning to think: quiet times for reflection, free periods for observation, games which encourage problem solving.
- Mindfulness: the joy of just being, living in the moment.
- By learning to love, to enjoy being loved and to explore sexuality in a healthy way.

School Enlightenment Programme: the Basic Theme of a New Age Curriculum

Philosophers since the time of Descartes have struggled to comprehend the nature of consciousness and embody its essential properties. Research issues of interest include phenomena such as perception, subliminal thoughts, blindsight, anosognosia (lack of insight), brainwaves during sleep and altered states of consciousness produced by psychoactive drugs, or spiritual or meditative techniques.

What might a higher level of consciusness look like? We all know there are altered levels of consciousness some of which we all experience, sleep for instance or anaesthetic sedation. Loss of consciousness after head trauma or recreational drugs taken specifically to alter levels of consciousness seem to affect certain brain areas which are necessary for maintaining it.

New Age Education Programme

The most important thing to realise is that our present time is the most important. The <u>now</u> is key. The theme of the MidPoint stage of Evolution is to make sense of our existence and to enjoy our dynamic place within it. The key word of the MidPoint is <u>sufficiency</u>: to understand it, to use it. We are all at the <u>now</u> point in our Evolution and all we know is sufficient for our needs. Absolute knowledge does not exist for us at this point.

We each feel a need to establish our own identity within our social circles, to nurture the essence of ourselves in order to develop, be the best we can be. Be assured that you are an important part of the evolutionary process, that you have been "fitted in" as an integral part of all that is, equipped with all you require for your perpetual progress. It is good to know our special place, to accept this identity. We humans set upon ourselves a range of inhibitors, leaving us open to fear, confusion, neuroses and psychoses; however, by understanding and accepting this essential truth, we will find negative emotions such as insecurity, inadequacy, inferiority diminish as no one person is in more danger than another. We are all inter-related and inter-dependent. If man decides to repudiate this Intelligence, is he not abusing his gift of reason, designed to help him adjust to conflict, to develop a higher consciousness and personal fulfilment? Such misreasoning can only bring disorganisation, corruption, danger and death.

A new birth of thinking and feeling is necessary. The truth of the evolutionary question is within ourselves. All knowledge relating to its laws, principles, purpose is there and in order to know ourselves and our direct relationship with the Intelligence, humankind must first understand the defences that blind it to its own reality and its environment, which paralyses ego growth. We must discover the unconscious intelligence at work within us and learn to listen. We must learn to feel as well as to reason. We must learn to recognise the things that shape conscious knowingness to help us enjoy the pursuit of truth. It is only when we are renewed in the spirit that we can know the way of life, be part of that way of life, part of all that ever was, of what is, and of what will be. Only then will we be at one with, and fully directed by, the Philosophy of the Unconscious. It is a wondrous journey, this human thirst for knowledge never diminishes and it could be argued that with less universal conflict the passion for learning becomes heightened as everything becomes highly meaningful.

Publicly accessible knowledge has increased exponentially in recent decades, some used constructively but much used destructively, and within our schools of learning there is a decreased interest in pursuing original, artistic thought for its own sake, which impoverishes a society's cultural richness. Boundary free, ethical artistic explorations and collaborations are urgently required to build on the strengths and knowledge amassed, to help create the next stage of human maturity – a global aspirational shared economy of knowledge where every society can evolve its potential.

The biomedical and physical scientists and technologists must accept that the emotional and spiritual factors found within research cannot any longer be dismissed as unscientific and unworthy of serious consideration. If a scientist asks the right questions, there is a likelihood he will find an answer but if he goes on to test wider outcomes he may not comprehend the right answer from amongst the options even if it were present. Understanding mankind's connection with reality and our place in the share of life reinforces the significance of the <u>now</u>. The consequences of choosing to live without recognising our part in the rollout of Evolution are damaging us humans, disturbing our human emotions, our emotional health, endangering our spiritual growth.

The New Age education programme is holistic, covering three essential spectra:

- Education, to fit us for our future;
- Developing higher consciousness: bridging the gap between the world of human experience, the three-fold world of physical, emotional and mental functioning, and higher spiritual

development which is the world of intuitive perception, spiritual insight and understanding; and

• Development of our reasoning to make humans intelligent citizens, controlled personalities and wise parents.

The Lucis Trust, an organisation founded in the USA in the 1920s and dedicated to developing and encouraging the spread of spiritual practices to create a stable and interdependent world, suggests a similar set of priorities for New Age education:

"The general trend of the new education should, therefore, be more psychological than in the past and educators should in the future lay emphasis upon:

1. *A developing mental control of the emotional nature.*
2. *Vision or the capacity to see beyond what is, to what might be.*
3. *Inherited, factual knowledge upon which it will be possible to superimpose the wisdom of the future.*
4. *Capacity wisely to handle relationships and to recognise and assume responsibility.*
5. *The power to use the mind in two ways:*
   a) *As 'common sense', analysing and synthesising the information conveyed by the five senses.*
   b) *As a searchlight, penetrating into the world of Ideas and abstract truth.*

Finally, education should present the hypothesis of the soul in man as the interior factor which produces the good, the true and the beautiful."(www.lucistrust.org)

<u>Self and Others:</u>
We all gain knowledge from experience, by asking questions. A question is like a hook which drags up an answer. It is the experience of that <u>now</u> moment and our reaction to it, the intake factor, the assimilation factor and the point of gain of additional knowledge which is significant for us. Not just the understanding we gain, or the situation of the learning, it is the actual learning experience, that psychological <u>now</u> moment when knowledge is gained is the value. It is the emotional equivalent of an exclamation mark in text, a direct knowledge-gain symbol, an idea established, a new piece added to the jigsaw. The <u>now</u> is the very moment where everything happens: its happening, its assimilation, and the overall enrichment. It is the success story of each of our lives. Contained within the experience is also some hidden, unavailable truth, for it is seldom that a total revelation is revealed. The absolute truth eludes us all. Necessarily. It would be overwhelming otherwise and would not enable us to assimilate the experience.

So, we learn the lesson, live the experience. That in itself is sufficient to provide vital lessons, to learn the importance of listening totally, of observing carefully, of recording from the environment, gaining new ground, moving from comparative ignorance to greater knowledge.

We may choose to ask a question of another, or ask a question within ourselves. Whatever serves us best. Our soul knows which questions to ask. Each of us should be confident enough of ourselves that we will ask the right questions. We can extract a moment of wisdom externally for our hook or, from within pull our own white rabbit out of our own hat at that very <u>now</u> moment. That moment of revelation is our own personal step forward. It is our Evolution taking place, our individual psychic expression of Evolution. These are the forces that bring furtherance to our life programme, and no less to our individual souls. In the equilibrium of the moment, with the powerful use of our senses, the soul gains its greatest knowledge. It expands in all dimensions, in all essential aspects. It is a fascinating moment of reality when our own reality attaches to the external reality and becomes an evolutionary reality.

Ask the right question and you will get the right answer. <u>your</u> right answer, for your own personal gain. Not <u>the</u> answer, not the total answer. Your answer because you asked the question for your own individual self and can thus only obtain your answer for your own use, for the use of your soul.

Your soul is forever seeking out, ferreting out, the knowledge required to move a step forward out of ignorance. What could be more beautiful than that? That moment of truth? That inspirational moment, our own wonderful experience of an aspect of wondrous evolutionary reality?

Having acquired greater knowledge, we will want absolute truth, the complete answer to everything, an instant uptake of knowledge - but we want too much! It is a human weakness. We want to feel like a lucky man in a casino. We often choose in such an ill-advised manner, creating our own frustrations and disappointments in so doing. The lesson says men seek for a moon, other lands, all kinds of tantalising resources from their environment without growing, within themselves, parallel inner resources.

The truth is within ourselves.

Place importance on respect for inner instincts and understanding of our emotions. We have very many but do not need to manifest them all. We should be selective about which we draw on in order to fully develop ourselves.

Families should place importance on training each member of their family to be the best they can be, a holistic approach to personal growth: the body, mind and the soul. Families should be rewarded for, and should value, learning as the necessary tool to understanding

Child Development:
Small children in all societies are naturally naive, inquisitive beings fascinated by the world they experience around them. Their potential can be simply achieved through providing opportunities which stimulate their curiosity, expose them to philosophy and debate to encourage their thinking, develop their creativity, spirituality and senses

through exploring the widest range of art, music, literature, philosophy, sport and science.

The ego is a powerful central force of the inner world, strengthened by accumulated knowledge and personal creative development. The ego can be uplifted in substantive ways, often when comparisons have been unwittingly made by others and the person suddenly feels inadequate and is inspired to make him or herself "adequate" again. Of course, this is a wrong perception as that person was perfectly adequate all the time.

Chapter 5
Beyond the Self: Spiritual Truth, Unity, Order, Perfection

The better consciousness in me lifts me into a world where there is no longer personality and causality or subject or object, and my belief is that this super-sensible and extra-temporal consciousness will become my only one. For that reason I hope it is not God, but if anyone wants to use the name God symbolically for this consciousness itself, or for much that we are able to separate, or name, so let it be: yet not among philosophers I would have thought.

Arthur Schopenhauer, *The World as Will and Representation*, 1844

"Western consciousness has been separated from the unconscious and the latter is suppressed. Since one cannot detach oneself from something of which one is unconscious, the European must first know his subject" (Jung, *Abstracts of the Collected Works of C.G. Jung,1978*). It is premature to seek liberation from something we have no contact with. To try to do so will foster only a greater separation.

In the early 1820s Schopenhauer started to use the term *"the better consciousness"*, a consciousness that lies beyond all experience and thus all reason, both theoretical and practical, a flash of insight without necessarily understanding. Higher consciousness is consciousness of a higher self, transcendental reality, or god. It is part of the human being that is capable of transcending animal instincts described by Fichte, Hegel and Kant as part of the German Idealism movement in the mid 1700s whose philosophy was deemed to be a western reformulation of the eastern mystical teachings of Advaita.

Whilst there is no single definition among the widely differing different spiritual philosophies across the world which define behaviours which indicate one's attainment of higher consciousness, these are some of the most commonly agreed:

- Intensified perception in wakefulness.
- Increased ability to be in the present, a timelessness.

- Awareness of a presence, or all-pervading spiritual energy.
- Alertness, a feeling of harmony and connectedness with the world.
- Inner quietness.
- Transcendence of the separation between the conscious and the unconscious.
- Empathy and compassion.
- Physical, mental and emotional wellbeing.

Life is not an empirical phenomenon, it is whatever we experience at each moment. To be a living organism is the manifestation of the experience of being conscious and relating to the world in a particular way. Each has a different experience but all living beings of the same species have a similar enough experience so that they have the sense of understanding each other and do not function in isolation, yet each is different enough so there is still a capacity to be able to surprise each other. We live in a world based on consciousness, driven by will and intention, not denying our essential reality, our consciousness, instead considering our ability to observe and experience to be the reason that we exist.

Consciousness Beyond the Brain
Let us look at consciousness beyond the brain, to ongoing research into differences between the mind and the brain.

Valuation of self is named the ego. The ego is weakened and feels discomfort when the self feels emotions of inferiority, inadequacy, inefficiency or other negative emotions which do not permit feelings of satisfaction to surface. The ego is only strong when the self is developing harmoniously within and with its environment.

If all instincts have their expressions sublimated comfortably rather than repressed, then harmonious growth can continue as the ego probes outwards in its environment and readjusts satisfactorily. The biological helplessness of an infant creates some conflict situations which they are not able to resolve themselves. However, as they learn to overcome such situations without fear, the new-found pleasure of confidence is found. Their ego has grown healthily. Anxiety and fear experienced during this overcoming may cause energy to be used at first but a point will come when such achievements bring with them a release-feeling of mastery and on the next occasion a feeling of confidence or triumph will enable the solution to be effected more easily, and with greater awareness. However, when the self tries to overcome the conflict, but does not fully succeed, fear is created then later repressed causing impoverishment of the ego.

Our mental responses, unconscious mechanisms of our ego-defence, fall into many categories which may, or may not, achieve their intention:

- Rationalisation;
- Fantasy;
- Projection;
- Displacement/transference;
- Over-compensation;
- Undoing;
- Conversion;
- Denial;
- Isolation;
- Regression;
- Reaction Formation;
- Sublimation.

Defences which fail to defend the ego effectively and redirect unsatisfactorily are unsuccessful. Where defence is partial it remains unsuccessful, requiring further defence at a later stage. Sometimes a series of partial defences is staged, becoming a negative mental "habit". Such unsuccessful defences, by their very nature, produce an unreality which limits the ego's development, prevents full relaxation but inspires fatigue due to the amount of mental energy required by the defensive interplay of the unconscious mind.

Denial is the simplest form of defence. It is simply the use of a mental mechanism to imagine something which did not happen. *"I can't believe it's true!"* is a common expression.

Projection is a cleverer unconscious method by which the self can retain a comfortable ego, regardless of circumstances, by transferring the blame to something or someone external. In this way personal responsibility is repudiated, preventing the individual from facing disturbing facts that his failures were due to his own actions, and not the failings of others.

Introjection is a device by which false values are irrationally elevated by the go whilst stunting its emotional growth. An example: A young male patient of the author's was seen by him leaving the local library with a pile of textbooks under his arm. Later, it was discovered that he did not intend to read them. He "felt" like a scholar whilst he was in the library and this was sufficient for him and it boosted his ego. Later investigation revealed that whilst not having gained knowledge in a conventional academic way, he projected a fantasy-based persona in order to acquire the knowledge he felt he lacked, content with feeling like an intellectual student when carrying "knowledge" out of the library. It was as if possession of knowledge in a physical sense enabled him to possess it in a mental capacity.

It can be seen therefore that a combination of introjection and projection, as described here, can protect the ego, albeit in an unrealistic way. The "good" qualities are fantasised as already present and the "bad" qualities able to be repudiated through some other thing, or person, in this way, allowing the ego to remain intact.

Sublimation is an example of successful defence where energy is arrested in its original outflow and is passed into another socially acceptable, comfortable channel. As an example, for it to be ideal where sexual instincts have been repressed continually there is a need to find another outlet. Where the instinct is redirected but not desexualised it will become a perversion. In sublimating, one can sometimes achieve a higher level of desexualised self-expression as in the case of a male patient who, when retreating from a destructive relationship redirected his passion into music and in time became a successful composer.

Repression is a form of denial often used successfully. The energies involved being more dynamic a form of repudiation, it can serve a valuable purpose except and unless when valuable material needed by the mind is shut away permanently from our mental life. All mental components should contribute to our mental life and the development of our ego. When material needed for ego development is permanently inaccessible, then stunted personality traits are likely to occur.

Reaction formation is a common form of ego defence in which emotions and impulses which are anxiety-producing, or perceived to be unacceptable, are mastered by exaggeration (hypertrophy) of the directly opposing tendency, such as a passive-receptive person who represses feelings of aggression.

Defensiveness, Denial, Projection, Sublimation and Repression are not just behaviours of the individual, of course, but are also highly visible in the behaviours of leaders of nations, leaders of political parties, politicians and other guardians of people.

The Family Pattern
Historically, gestalt practitioners such as Fritz and Lore Perls and Paul Goodman have agreed that our conception of "the family" is based on "group behaviour". What, perhaps, has not been sufficiently acknowledged and is insufficiently applied in practical group psychology and therapy, is the reverse correlation: that group life is based on the family pattern.

The pattern for our very earliest co-operation, which plays so great a part in our society is the co-operation between mother and baby. This seems to be the right moment for saying that I believe our society is evolving to represent the mother-image, where immature individuals expect to be kept and fed by society (the mother) for some actually replacing a real mother figure. The more individuals reach maturity, the more they will co-operate with the "mother" society. This is borne out in dependency groups, like Alcoholics Anonymous, whose members manifest child-mother behaviours, typically saying *"I want society to give me back a little more than I can put in"*, *"I expect society to like/respect me"*, *"Society should provide for me, show friendliness and kindness, develop my possibilities"*.

How mothers bring up their children and how those children develop as adults is of the utmost importance for the society to which they belong. Alfred Adler (1870-1930) proposed: *"The mother has the enormous advantage of the physical and psychic relationship. She is the greatest experience of love and fellowship that the child will ever have. Her duty is mentally to relate the growing child to herself, nourishing the child's growing consciousness with true and normal conceptions of wider society, of work, and of love."*(Academy of Ideas, *Superiority, Inferiority and Courage*, 2017) In this way, she gradually transforms the child's love for her and dependence on her into a benevolent, confident, responsible attitude towards society, and wider human fellowship. Thus, the two-fold function of motherhood is to give the child the most complete experience of human fellowship and then to widen it into a life attitude towards others.

Inevitably, some modern families are ill-equipped emotionally, socially and financially to deal with the new stage, which will be detrimental to future generations, dooming their societies to continued social stagnation or disorder and an unnecessary limitation on their potential development.

Stable families encapsulate all the emotion of a shared domain, distancing itself from matters and outside influences which distract it from developing a strong unity. The family is therefore a training workshop stage where emotional, mental and physical development happens in familiar, known ways. We only learn the next lesson we need when we are ready to learn. The baby will learn to use a spoon with his hands only when he or she is ready. In the same way it is pointless expecting that newborn to eat from a plate. We are all of us, at this precise moment, on the brink of learning our own next lesson, whatever it may be. It is the same for every person.

Early New Age education about Evolution will tend to keep the soul in its basic equilibrium, so even if there is a traumatic imbalance or disturbance, the child will more easily regain equilibrium. There will be less chance of drastic traumatic disturbance from which the individual may suffer prolonged imbalance and mental, even physical, disturbances.

Living life is not an easy, comfortable journey. Somewhere along the way, as experience progresses and learning happens one event after another, we realise that our first impressions, those established truths, our early reactions to our environment, might not actually constitute objective truths.

It is obvious that what we think life is about will colour our outlook and our behaviour. Our outlooks, the beliefs we hold will influence our conduct, our understanding of the world, and how we react to its challenges. If we believe life is good and we are part of that, when we wake in the mornings we expect that interesting things may happen and this, in turn, will shape our attitudes and our behaviours.

We are creatures of multiple emotions, some positive and beneficial others negative and harmful. We are like electronic apparatus activated and sustained by dynamic instincts with all the power of the creative intelligence of life firing us, and our behaviour will reflect the degree of progress we have made in developing, stabilising, and utilising our inner creative power to seek our truths.

But what is truth? In fact there are three kinds of truth. There is subjective truth: what a person believes to be true based on their own experiences and their reactions to it. An embodiment, we could say. There is objective truth: truth based on all facts available. A legalistic or scientific approach perhaps? Then there is absolute truth which represents the physical and spiritual reality of creation.

Awareness of each of these truths is a fundamental element of any spiritual education and I suggest should be integral to developing a rounded personality, if we are to raise intelligent, enquiring, caring, competent children

Equally, failing to understand our environment in its own context limits the countryside to just being a pretty bucolic backdrop or a challenging wilderness to be conquered in some way and city landscapes to being urban jungles to be afraid of. The real wonders of our natural environment and its natural history, are ever present and everlasting. They have entranced and fascinated our children at each stage of their learning but have never been understood to be a key element of our living environment, our eco-culture, which would enrich our understanding of our place on this planet, and beyond it. This already accessible genre of learning should be expanded to include evolutionary biology and physics as an integral part of primary education to orient the emergence from early infantile learning through stories and rhymes with their contrived moralities and dark undertones towards a more acceptable understanding for young people of their physical environment, and their place within it.

Our pre-MidPoint society may find this unpalatable, undoable, unimportant. The family as a model for nurturing potential has been abused, is unsupported, the role having been delegated to schools, television programmes and social networks. The modern family has increasingly become a breeding ground for self-centred, anti-loving, anti-social behaviour and has become dysfunctional. Parenting is not now socially valued and is barely resourced. Young adults are given no preparation to help them plan their families, their lives, their own development, their place in the world.

However, despite this resistance, it is imperative that we move towards New Age methods of nurturing and education, not just for the sake of individuals, but, more collectively, because it will provide generations of societies with a common motivation to contribute towards building a collaborative, mutually respectful, civilising civilisation without which our species cannot endure.

Critiques of New Age Education

Unsurprisingly, religious and mainstream educational providers in the West have been slow to relinquish their controls over the spiritual and social mentoring of our young.

New Age philosophy is roundly rejected by Creationists who consider only Biblical teachings capable of ushering in a perfect society. (Eric Buehrer, *The New Age Masquerade: The Hidden Agenda in Your Child's Classroom*, Wolgemuth and Hyatt, 1990)

Other theologians have seen parallels between New Age Spiritualism and Progressive Christianity, identifying five indicators:

1. Redefinition or the Abandonment of the Concept of Sin: New Agers believe that all people are inherently divine, that there is no such thing called sin but only the failure to remember our divinity, their mantra being that there is no sin, the Atonement is the final lesson a person needs to learn for it teaches that never having sinned we are in no need of Salvation.

2. The Denial of Absolute Truth: A distinctive feature of progressive Christianity is its denial of biblical authority, but few of us choose to operate without an authority. If you remove one you will replace it with another. Typically, Progressive Christians shift the authority for

what they believe is true from the Bible to themselves, becoming their own moral compass, which will inevitably adapt to reflect their own time and culture.

3. Acceptance of Jesus but denial of his blood atonement: New Age thought leaders almost always couch their teachings in Christian language. Jesus is an example of someone who attained enlightenment by connecting with the divine, offering an example that any of us can follow. His death wasn't a "saving" act in itself as the saving comes from within ourselves as we realise we have within us the same capabilities as Jesus. This is often referred to as Christ Consciousness, thus the eucharist ceremony is less an atonement than a ritual to heighten our senses to our bonds with our brothers and sisters in our shared humanity.

4. It's All About Me: New Age thought revolves around the self: self-empowerment and realisation of our innate divinity are central to its teachings and practices. Progressive teacher Richard Rohr proclaims that each of us, and sometimes "creation", is the fourth member of the blessed Trinity, implying the fullness of divinity isn't complete until we become part of it.

5. Universalism: New Age proponents affirm the idea that all roads lead to the divine. Its movement holds tightly to religious pluralism

and universalism, which is the view that all religions are inspired by a common source and they all point to the same Truth that we will all inevitably reach, regardless of what path we choose to get there: Universal Salvation.

Brooks Alexander (*Forward* magazine, Autumn 1986) proclaimed more forcefully: *"In the biological contest for cultural supremacy, public education is the prime target: it influences the most people in the most pervasive way, at the most impressionable age. No other institution has anything close to the same potential for mass indoctrination."*

Thus, New Age teachings have been seen by some as skewed meditative practices. New Age education has been perceived as unethical, masquerading academic, psychological or scientific teachings. There were concerns that it was transgressive psychic intervention intended to overrule children's and their parents' rights to follow conventional learning programmes.

Similarly, The Watchman Fellowship, an independent Christian research and apologetics ministry that focuses on religious movements, cults, the occult and the New Age, has this to say:

"The New Age is deemed to be part of an insidious anti-Christian movement using visualisation and medication to influence young minds in schools to open their minds to spiritual influences, which may be dangerous to their mental and emotional health. There are

some 300 programmes being taught across the USA to create generations of New Age teachers."

Of course, any education based on current popular knowledge and social trends will base its structures on standardised conformist theories so that students of that teaching will receive only stereotyped, partisan teachings. Any person breaking that mould will likely be considered to be ineducable and rebellious by that teaching regime, perhaps even being thought a threat to the establishment.

Steve Deckard, of the Institute for Creation Research, writes as follows:

"Ideas are important. They shape our behaviour, our philosophy of life and, ultimately, our world view. One such set of ideas promoted in educational circles is called Global Education.

Proponents may disguise it by using other names: Multicultural education, futurism, Project 2000, World Core Curriculum.

Advocates of this philosophy support four basic principles:

1. *Everyone should become involved with people of other cultures.*

2. *From earliest childhood, global studies should be involved in all areas of study.*

3. *Economic interdependence among all peoples and nations should be stressed.*

4.   *The changing role of individual nationals should be emphasised, highlighting the increasing importance of international organisations.*

On the surface some of these may seem acceptable but beneath lies a programme of cultural evolution designed to swallow up national and personal identities

By undermining cultural, religious, national and economic distinctions, the stage is being set for the alternative: A synthetic, unified system. This new world religion is envisaged as a synthesis of Christian ethics and Eastern mysticism, in which the task of reordering our traditional values and institutions is given over to our state schools. This type of thinking could produce a climate ripe for a charismatic one-world leader, whom the Bible calls the Anti-Christ."

Scientists calling for a paradigm shift in which events are viewed holistically and in which scientific laws, constructs and views of how the human mind thinks and functions are redefined, are marine biologist James Lovelock and microbiologist Lynn Margulis. Both strongly advocate the Gaia Hypothesis, in which the earth is compared to a living entity with humanity as a part of its life system. It has spawned a new science which Lovelock calls Geophysiology.

This has been taken by Creationist and anti-New Age critics as suggesting that it is possible for the earth and humanity to leave behind their ills and move into the Utopian situation. That Utopia will supersede the present world of environmental and wartime crises and will usher in an era of life in oneness with nature and a community at peace with its neighbours. In this New Age there will be one universal religion expressed through other local religions, and there will be an allegiance to the planet and the human race that will supersede loyalties to the more limited groupings of clan, race or region.

However, although such claims have been attributed to Lovelock, he himself is quite clear that "Gaia" is a metaphor, and he does not relate it to New Age ideas and universal religions – though other later writers have (mis)-interpreted it that way, and he has subsequently stated: *"Nowhere in our writings do we express the idea that planetary self-regulation is purposeful, or involves foresight or planning by the biota."* While the Gaia theory was the first and perhaps only cohesive proposal that all the living systems are deeply intertwined, his perception of humankind's response to it is more dystopian than many other writers on the subject. This is alluded to in his statement on global warming:*"We have all the things needed to stop global warming but we just don't use them."*(James Lovelock speaking on *Green Originals*, BBC Radio 4, 13 January 2020).

Rabindranath Tagore, acclaimed universal philosopher, artist and Nobel Prize Winner for Literature pursued a lifelong interest in education, leading him to found both a school and a university. His ideal was the Universal Human Being: a rational, humane, creative and spiritual soul, as he deemed himself.

Tagore keenly felt the social corruptions and restrictions of his (Indian) society and challenged them all without resorting to a prevailing belief in the West being the source of all evil. He welcomed Western science, particularly belief in individual worth, freedom and democracy. In his writings he emphasised his cherished values: unity in diversity, harmony, creativity and interiority.

He saw man as *"the angel of surplus, since the spirit of man has an enormous surplus far in excess of the requirements of the biological animal in man"*(*The Religion of Man*, 1931). Civilisation is therefore the product of surplus in man. Science, religion, art, philosophy are all made possible by this surplus.

His school, named Shantiniketan (The Abode of Peace) was modelled on the ancient hermitage schools of India which emphasised the importance of children's awareness of nature, of sensitivity of soul in their relationships with human surroundings through festive ceremonials, prolific literature and spiritual teachings, enjoining them *"to attain the presence of the world through the soul, thus to gain more than can be measured – like gaining an instrument in truth by bringing out its music."*

Group Dynamics and National Identities

It is worth observing here that the structures and symbols of group behaviours also exist within nations. The intellectual growth of any nation will be limited by that nation's collective political and religious aspirations for its citizenry. The political energy of the people will reflect their response to the parenting style of their government, through their patriarchal or matriarchal behaviours. The former have been clearly observable in nations as diverse as Germany and Russia, North Korea and China, Syria and UEA, where the father figure develops an ascendency of power, imposing his will, his strength, his protection on society (the mother figure), while she is occupied with rearing her children. In contrast, in the USA, there has been a marked resistance to the autocracy of father-figures. Here a father is looked upon as the executive arm of the mother, whom her children regard as the centre of the family.

Ultimately, societies depend upon mothers for their future citizens and we can recognise how important it is that mothers' roles should be respected lest they bequeath their own sense of disappointment and dissatisfaction to their children. In societies where women are debased, that society is debased; where she is valued for her values and her enlightenment that society will be proportionately elevated - to expand her mental freedom is to enlarge and enrich her whole community.

Where equilibrium between the father and mother figures is balanced it provides a family, a gestalt group or a nation state with an integrated approach, a maturity, a higher degree of consciousness which elevates all within it and reduces underlying resistance and social imbalance.

An accepted therapeutic definition of an individual's personality is: *"the dynamic organisation within an individual of those psycho-physical systems that determine his* (sic) *characteristics, behaviour and thoughts."*(Gordon Allport, *Trait Theory,* 1961).

A therapeutic group usually consists of six or seven people, which also equates to an average Western family size and, as with any "family group gestalt", its incompleteness and gaps must be rounded off and filled with psychological insights, in the same way that individual adjustments must take place.

Gestalt psychotherapists will also attribute groups with the trait of personality, rationalising that one of the purposes of a group is for individuals to realise themselves within or through the group. By so combining their efforts, they achieve a group personality. A united and loyal community which lives a coherent life is, in a perfect literal sense, a living entity, individual personalities having become integrated in a group by achieving a common denominator of their characteristics. In this way, they also form *"a dynamic organisation of psycho-physical systems"* that determine its unique adjustment to the environment.

The first step in the formation of the group feeling amounts usually to mutual stock taking, a mutual search for emotional and mental similarities so as to engender feelings of security but it is usually a complicated process.

In a therapeutic group where all the members share a particular common aim, the need to make adjustments to find security within the group is usually unnecessary due to the presence of a group leader, in whom the members find a centre to whom they can transfer their hopes. If he is a man, he will soon become a father-image which, given the patriarchal family structure of our society, is usually felt to represent security and will be expected to guide, maybe even to "discipline" group members. Any pathological infantile tendencies, originating from any early disappointment in demands for security, may manifest. Group members will re-enact parts psycho-dramatically which they have already played as young children in accordance with their original family patterns, transferring their emotions not only to the father-analyst but to members of the groups who take over the parts of brothers and sisters. They co-operate by acting together and thus become more integrated, experiencing the difficulties of adjustment – which may make up the central problem of a neurotic person – rather better than in individual therapy.

Equally, both individual and group personalities can be divided into the three accepted elements of mind: the id, the ego and the superego, the three distinct yet separate agents in the psychic apparatus defined in Freud's structural model of the psyche.

The group's endeavours towards a common aim are related to the id; the aspects controlling the endeavours which are represented by the father/leader and mother/group who represent the group identity are the ego; the superego is expressed in the use of "we" which indicates acceptance of the endeavours undertaken on the group's behalf.

Whilst an individual's ego structure is reinforced by belonging to a "we" structure, it can also be endangered if individuals' tendencies are overlooked. It would, on the whole, approach the group ideal if the individual personality can be brought into accord with the group personality. The formation of a group personality appears to me to be due to an adjustment of the individuals towards one another on the one hand, and towards the group as a superego on the other. Once an adjustment between the id, the ego and the superego is attained, one can speak of an integrated, harmonious and normal group personality.

It is the adjustment to one another, so very necessary, which is the individual's emotional problem and one which can cause upheavals both in the person and in group communities. Every group tends to form a community in the truest sense of the word, being a gathering together of people with common aims.

The two-fold adjustment towards each other and towards the group is reached by the projection of one's own superego onto the members of the group at the same time as some outside stimulation is felt upon the whole group. It takes place in order that fear may be avoided and security found, a security without which no group feeling, or any other social relationship, can be achieved. As with the organs of an organised body, so must the organs of an organism find their assured place within. This they do by upholding their own individual value whilst, at the same time, supporting the other organs in a joint pursuit of the constructive benefits of life.

"For most of us love is the most absorbing subject in existence. There is an enormous range of meanings in this one little word: mother and father love, self love, children's love for their parents, love of one's home and one's country, love of money, love of power, love of god - but the love in which one can be is the most pre-eminent love for most of us. Love, at its fullest, can include an enormous range of emotions and sentiments. It can combine humility with pride, passion with peace, self-assertion with self-surrender, reconcile violence with tenderness, sublimate sexual desire into joy, and the realisation of a fuller life." (Julian Huxley, *Essays of a Humanist*,1961).

Ideally, every family should receive financial and social support from the state for the first four years of its being to provide a relaxed environment within which parents will work on creating strong bonds with their children and other family members, to realise their own strengths and understand their academic, creative and spiritual potential, to establish their place within their own community and in the wider world with the final intention of creating the perfect launch pad for their children to achieve their potential.

If we can accept Evolution as our guide we can dispense with man-made mythologies about gods and supernatural powers. Isn't that what we have all been seeking? To understand what life is about. A realisation that we have always been part of existential life, and always will be? Won't we have found our rightful place?

This profound realisation forms the basis of New Age education such as I have promised and it is most suitable for developing a universal, secular programme for learning which recognises and expands our understanding in all scientific spiritual, artistic and communitarian arenas of knowledge. It is the essential and most timely education programme and eminently suited to this MidPoint time. Its time is now!

Chapter 6
How the New Age Spiritual Family Can Rally To Save Humankind

A developed human being is not merely a more highly individualised individual, he has crossed the threshold of self-consciousness to a new mode of thought. As a result he has achieved some degree of conscious integration — integration of the self with the outer world of men and nature, integration of the separate elements of the self with each other. He is a person, an organism which has transcended individuality in personality. This attainment of personality is an essential element in man's past and present evolutionary success: accordingly, its fuller achievement must be an essential aim for his evolutionary future.

Pierre Teilhard de Chardin, *The Phenomenon of Man,*
1955

Humankind is, in the Freudian sense, becoming adult for the first time, having the knowledge to behave maturely, capable of reaching its collective potential as a member of the New Age global community. Each individual is able to contribute to the wider group's sustenance by sharing knowledge and experience with all those who wish to hear, to provide communities, families and their children with opportunities to achieve their potential for their own personal growth as well as the enrichment of the wider group. Such an expansionist, universal approach to educating ourselves and our future generations requires freedom. Freedom of thought, freedom to act in the interests of ourselves and of others; but such freedom needs to be tempered with compassion and integrity if it is to benefit society as a whole.

Evolution, as a manifestation of its natural laws, underlies the development of the universe according to a pre-determined plan. The processes of Evolution operate at a number of different levels, not just biological, as in the formation and adaptation of species but also in the lives of individual humans and the development of groups, societies and cultures. In addition, there is a spiritual dimension to human development which needs to be acknowledged and nurtured in order for the overall evolutionary plan to unfold in the optimum way for humankind.

The laws which underpin the processes of Evolution are at present only partly understood, and the discovery and application of these laws to human life, relationships and societies would assist in the optimal development of the evolutionary plan.

The lack of recognition and understanding of these laws in this current pre-MidPoint stage has led to a situation of chaos in the psychological and emotional lives of individuals, and in relationships between individuals and groups, societies and nations, which impedes the progress of the evolutionary plan.

The MidPoint of Evolution is the stage in which the chaos of the pre-MidPoint begins to be resolved, creating the conditions for Evolution to progress to the next, inevitable and supremely better stage, the New Age. The speed of this transition can be improved by a better understanding and application of evolutionary laws, and this should be the main priority of individuals and societies.

Further, the fragmentation of fields of study into distinct disciplines and diverse religious doctrines has led to polarisation within areas of shared knowledge, which has hindered the very development of understanding the Laws of Evolution necessary for progress between the pre-MidPoint, the MidPoint and the New Age. As such, the reintegration and sharing of knowledge at the highest level should be considered our first priority.

A major block within the pre-MidPoint stage is the problem of opposites: a tendency to create polarities such as right and wrong, light and dark, love and hate, perfection and imperfection, which leads to a sense of extremism and conflict rather than creating an environment in which opposing categories are seen as elements on a spectrum.

In the late fourteenth century, the English term "freedom" (according to the OED) meant: "*Exemption from arbitrary or despotic control: civic liberty.*" By 1570, it had expanded its meaning to include "*the possession of particular privileges*" – thus, freedom from abusive action implied now the ability to act in certain free ways oneself. When Shakespeare in Titus Andronicus has Bassanius say "*Romans, fight for freedom in your choice*", he means fighting for the right to both things.

However, unlimited freedom demands no enablement and its very lack of constraints consumes itself in chaos. The libertines described by the Marquis de Sade boasted of unconstrained freedom, obeying neither the laws of nature, nor those of society, but limited freedom is not necessarily restricted to the freedom framed by the rule of societal law, it can also mean the legislation of self-restraint and individual ethics.

Today we separate freedom and freedom's worth: that is to say, the nominal right to freedom and the right to act according to that freedom. One can apply this to freedom of speech, of thought, of belief but by acting on those freedoms, the libertines demonstrated to unbearable lengths that we humans are capable of anything. Only our imagination limits the inventiveness of our crimes. The tortured and desecrated bodies strewn along the pages of the Marquis's books are less a proof of the freedom to act than a proof of the lack of a framework for that assumed freedom. That is what is thought to be behind Plato's declaration in *The Laws* that:*"a limited freedom is far better than an unlimited one."*

Creationists wrongly assume that Evolutionism contradicts the three Laws of Thermodynamics, namely the physical quantities of temperature, energy and entropy. Our planet's system, whether we talk about life, rainfall or photosynthesis, is finally dependent on the steady flow of energy we receive from the sun. Whilst never actually disobeying the laws of chemistry and physics, energy from the sun powers life, coaxes the laws of physics and chemistry to evolve prodigious feats of complexity, beauty, diversity and uncanny illusions of statistical improbability and deliberate design.

The author of the Gaia Hypothesis, scientific visionary James Lovelock, presented a radical vision of humanity's future in his series of books, particularly in *A Rough Ride to the Future* (2014), in which he postulated that in the 1700s humanity entered a new age, the Anthropocene, which will culminate in it - it being us and our descendants - having the pivotal role in the all-enveloping world of artificial intelligence as we become *"the thinking brain of our Earth system"*.

Even the ultimate nay-sayers, the existentialists, acknowledged that humanism validates the human subject as struggling for self-knowledge and self-responsibility. Jean-Paul Sartre believed existentialism to be humanism because it expressed the power of human beings to make freely-willed choices, independent of the influence of religion or society. Unlike traditional humanisms, however, Sartre disavowed any reliance on the essential nature of man deriving values from the facts of human nature. Rather he saw human value as self-created through undertaking projects in living and experimenting in the world.

Albert Camus, in *The Plague* (1947), suggests that some of us may choose to be heroic even while knowing it will bring us neither reward nor salvation.

Simone de Beauvoir, in *The Ethics of Ambiguity* (1948): *"embraced our own personal freedom which requires us to fight for the freedoms of all humanity"*.

So, how do we go about replicating the best characteristics of homo sapiens to create a future in which we can all thrive and bring the collective benefits of shared understanding to our communities and future generations? It is a huge task requiring many to change their mindset, reject narrow parochialism, embrace old and new learnings for the benefit of future humankind. It is both aspirational and admirable but will demand cultural liberalism which many people, organisations and countries will find challenging.

My aim in writing this book has been to show in the most simple, non-scientific language, that we have reached the MidPoint in our civilisation: where we do have sufficient knowledge to collectively synthesise a New Age in human history. We already have the knowledge, and already share enough common direction, to be able to create such a humanitarian model of society in which we will all thrive but we must first urgently find peaceable ways to overcome the human imperative to conquer one another!

Man has good cause to be afraid of conventional political centres of power as, if left unchallenged, unilateral directions come eventually to serve only themselves, leading to corruption, oppression and violence. But a centralised movement could equally be harnessed to act for the good of the planet, of its society, with academics from every discipline being put in place at every level of education to share knowledge, inculcate a pride in achieving individual potential both to enrich the individual but also to make a contribution to society, to undertake new research and achieve a common purpose among students of diverse backgrounds, each contributing as they are able for the benefit of others.

We seek to be proud of our nation, Great Britain, and we become distressed when it does not live up to its name. There are no inspiring solutions either from governments or any other institutions for a forward looking ideal for developing an exciting, dynamic model global community. It cannot be just a Utopian dream, idealistic but unachievable.

In our efforts to establish democracy we have rejected feudal, omnipotent and autocratic leaderships in favour of freedom of thought and speech, challengeable legislation, elections and consensus – and this has led to division and conflict.

We can, and must, create a future for mankind: a way or route scalable enough that population masses can follow. Can we halt current levels of disorder and chaos to establish a movement that can make progress without generating fear, tackle uncertainty with a vision of consensus?

This failing is remediable. It is that we have not harnessed the energy, creativity, intellectual capacity of our citizens, who are not united together for any common purpose.

We therefore need to establish a new structure for harmonious learning, living and loving. In Western societies today there are few fundamental rules for living together. Anything goes. Fear arises from perceiving danger, unpredictability. Disturbance indicates loss of internal peace and harmony, disorder is a manifestation of physical and mental change within, anxiety is often born of a person's fear of a lack of control over their life experiences.

The New Age philosophy should not be overlooked any longer. It is an ideal model, spiritual yet prosaic, for truth-accepting, open-minded, mature citizens who can, and will, contribute something positive and dynamic towards developing their society's future. Humanity, compassion and truth must prevail to underpin a harmonious and socially integrated model for learning and living with purpose and order giving it direction. It is thus that I propose the family, in any and all its forms, should be hailed for its importance in developing, educating, socialising its future generations. Their very future depends on our ability to teach them what is important. If we do not know why we are here, what we should be doing, why we should be doing it, where we came from, where we are going, we lack the essential knowledge, essential truths, to override half truths, superstitions, false beliefs.

The Role of the Spiritual Family

Whilst marriages are often made for the wrong psychological reasons: possessiveness, security, prestige, wealth, affluence or sex, and psychologists and therapists everywhere will attest to this, the existence in most cultures of the nuclear or extended family is the model for a balanced society.

Over a quarter of a million babies are born every day, which is nearly 100 million every year, born into a society where there is political, social and economic uncertainty and indecision, and no all-inclusive spiritual structure for living. Although it is accepted by many religions that each baby reborn is more advanced than in previous rebirths, the rules and controls of the prevailing society have a powerful environmental effect on the development of the child as it strives to grow.

The family encapsulates all the emotion of a shared domain, distancing itself from outside influences which distract it from developing a strong unity. The family is therefore a training workshop stage where emotional, mental and physical development happens in familiar, known ways. We only learn the next lesson we need when we are ready to learn. The baby will learn to use a spoon with his hands only when he or she is ready. In the same way that it is pointless expecting that newborn to eat from a plate, we are all of us, at this precise moment, on the brink of learning our own next lesson, whatever it may be. It is the same for every person.

The family is the consolidation of potentially perfect relationships set in motion by Evolution, whose first rule when any temporary loss of equilibrium is observed is to gently ease to restore the balance. Each family is a special, perfectly formulated group, a preparation stage, as all evolutional stages are, for the socialisation of the newborn into its group society. It is a family unity of souls, all motivated innately for the same procreative function in the scheme of life. That family is unique and emotionally self-contained, backed by all the evolutionary drives and energies required to ensure the perpetuation of creativity. Each member of the group quickly becomes emotionally connected to the others as they are sharing the experiences each is having. Emotions are powerful and instinctive but are driven by selfish reasons. As with games where participants must know and adhere to the rules or be disqualified, so society often determines that man's progress will be limited by its rules and norms. Defaulters are duly punished, maybe isolated, even removed from its influence to protect the wider group from the infection of unwanted ideas and behaviours. Any break in the social equilibrium of togetherness is not easily tolerated. Couples must be mature enough, fully engaged and emotionally ready to take such a responsibility if the soul, the mind and the body of a healthy baby is to be achieved. Each family then must become a teacher, trained in the exciting experience of family development: parenting skills, education.

When a baby completes its embryonic stage of growth and is born, it joins its outside world. It begins its next stage, entering the preparatory stage for the adult one that will follow. At the same time that baby is born, thousands of other babies are also being born. Families evolve everywhere, thriving units if happy, love-filled unity of being and purposes: a unique togetherness, which is difficult to describe.

The soul is in equilibrium at the very beginning of earthly life. Study the peace and tranquillity interrelationship between baby and mother as the baby's soul links up with the new environment, which may be startlingly different from earlier lives. A new, vital stage indeed.

Children must not be sent out into a confused world to work out the rules and responsibilities of belonging to it. Well laid-down plans of life and human loving and living must be taught to children as soon as they can understand, in ways they can understand otherwise the growing child will receive experiences from its environment causing him or her to worry that they are unsatisfactory in some way, below society's requirement. This is an unnecessary and disturbing experience, often based on perception rather than reality, but which can bring loss of equilibrium.

Instead of teaching them about tooth fairies, Father Christmas, bogey men, anthropomorphised cuddly animals which behave like humans and other fantasy creations, teach them about who and what they are, separate from being part of mum and dad.

Teach them how they came to be and illustrate the potential for themselves by mentoring them to achieve their intellectual, emotional and spiritual potential during their period of physical growth and maturity. Children should be taught about the continuum of stages of Evolution to understand that each stage has a lifecycle which needs to complete before it can merge into the stage to follow. For us humans there is a need to explore and mature a wide range of sensibilities if we are to develop emotionally and socially, to be considered, courageous and responsible in our behaviour, to be able to give or receive respect, love, comradeship and inspiration to within our peer groups. The emotional intelligence of the New Age family generates a love of living, of life itself, of others sharing our life and a sympathetic, empathetic desire to become a proactive member of the family unit. Such a family unit is indeed the natural model for life. No New Age child will want to run away from their family home!

Equally, teach them to navigate the practical challenges of living in a changing physical environment as rural settings are increasingly becoming urbanised but where the countryside is valued for itself as the birthplace of all life forms, not just as a pretty backdrop to have a picnic in or a challenging wilderness to be conquered.

Children love videos and films and these provide elements of education in an attractive audio-visual way but there is an absence of emphasis on any family-love attitudes, nor the wonders and beauties of nature and our place within it. Surprisingly few films, plays and stories acknowledge or celebrate the beauty of the love and support provided by family to its members, and particularly its children and young people. This inevitably provides a distorted reality for inexperienced minds. The family must become the focal point of our human development, become a stage of training which is essential to humankind's happiness and ultimately its survival.

Will this not be fascinating for the young adult to reflect on, a sound basis for his or her creative growth during adulthood, to fulfil the innate driving force within to achieve their ultimate potential?

The urge to maintain love-generating relationships is always a powerful force but mothers sometimes have difficulties in loving their own children, which may be due to the inhibition of loving feelings within themselves from early childhood, often an absence of rich emotional bonding in the first five years. Parents may need to be taught how to love their babies and how to respond to the baby's love for them. A child must learn about love in its first formative years, long before any thoughts of adult sexuality appears in life's curriculum.

Babies come into the world with a full set of emotions able to communicate fully with their parents and for parents lacking early maternal love they can take the lead from their baby. There should be no blame on the parents who have an understanding of their family's needs but may lack the knowledge or confidence to emote. Listening to their babies will enable them to create their own time together, their own emotional space. Their lack of experience is not a fault, it is an opportunity. Human communications are evolutionarily complex.

New Age teaching programmes have a mind-body focus which encourages the development of cognitive, emotional, spiritual and social understanding. More collectively, it will provide generations of societies with a common motivation to contribute towards building a collaborative, mutually respectful civilising civilisation without which our species cannot endure.

The pleasure I derive from learning my next lesson is exactly the same kind of pleasure the baby experiences when it discovers that it can hold its own rattle. Its knowledge is opening up, its consciousness is increased at that point. Adults too continue learning, though unbeknown there is an additional baseline of memory and experience from all that has been learned before in past lives and previous cultures. We do not start from zero. It brings a unique richness to our present moment. Families working together to achieve higher levels of creative development will transcend the limitations of former lives to achieve their personal and collective potential.

Evolution has a past and a future but the absolute reality is just what is at that point in time. There is nothing "good" about what it is, it just is. Equally, there is nothing "bad" about it. In the ideal nurturing setting of the New Age family, no child would ever be rejected, abused, antagonised, aggressive. Knowledge generates understanding and acceptance, leading to enlightenment, then wisdom. Families working together to achieve higher levels of creative development will transcend the limitations of former lives to achieve their personal and collective potential.

On leaving the pre-MidPoint stage of Evolution, the prevailing mantra for self-determination of "mind over matter" became open for discussion and the MidPoint concept of "spirit over mind" generally began to emerge. As we attune to the now completely we will relate to the creative interactions of spirit and mind.

New Age teaching programmes have a mind-body focus which encourages the development of cognitive, emotional, spiritual and social understanding. Many independent schools adhere to its philosophy but they are too rare. I ask why do we perpetuate school curricula which support social, educational and spiritual division? Now is the time to share our knowledge and respect other cultures in order to create an aspirational, harmonious movement which celebrates our humanity, our capacity to learn, to change and to improve our world the best ways we can to provide a safe and nurturing environment for future generations.

These are the cornerstones of our growth and should become the integrated foundation, the blueprint for our children's, and their children's learning, through which our society's future can be secured.

Humankind must act now to harness its innate creative inner resources, its resourcefulness, and its undeniable position on this planet, to develop a positive, nurturing humanity through which we share for everyone's good the huge body of knowledge, of irrefutable scientific facts and evidences, our social, cultural understandings and spiritual insights and blend these into educational programmes which stimulate every person to achieve their potential.

Printed in Poland
by Amazon Fulfillment
Poland Sp. z o.o., Wrocław

60881023R00101